UNDERSTANDING WISDOM LITERATURE

Understanding Wisdom Literature

Conflict and Dissonance in the Hebrew Text

David Penchansky

WILLIAM B. EERDMANS PUBLISHING COMPANY

GRAND RAPIDS, MICHIGAN / CAMBRIDGE, U.K.

Published 2012 by
Wm. B. Eerdmans Publishing Co.
2140 Oak Industrial Drive N.E., Grand Rapids, Michigan 49505 /
P.O. Box 163, Cambridge CB3 9PU U.K.
www.eerdmans.com

Printed in the United States of America

18 17 16 15 14 13 12   7 6 5 4 3 2 1

Library of Congress Cataloging-in-Publication Data

Penchansky, David.

Understanding wisdom literature: conflict and dissonance in the Hebrew text /
   David Penchansky.
        p.   cm.
   Includes bibliographical references.
   ISBN 978-0-8028-6706-3 (pbk.: alk. paper)
   1. Wisdom literature — Criticism, interpretation, etc.   I. Title.

BS1455.P36   2012
223′.06 — dc23

                                                      2011039558

Dedicated to my beloved wife, Hend Al-Mansour:

أنت عمري

أموت فيك

Contents

Abbreviations

AB	Anchor Bible
ABD	*Anchor Bible Dictionary*, ed. David Noel Freedman. 6 vols. New York: Doubleday, 1992
ABRL	Anchor Bible Reference Library
AnBib	Analecta biblica
APOT	*The Apocrypha and Pseudepigrapha of the Old Testament*, ed. R. H. Charles. 2 vols. Oxford: Oxford University Press, 1913
AYB	Anchor Yale Bible
BETL	Bibliotheca ephemeridum theologicarum lovaniensium
Bib	*Biblica*
BibInt	*Biblical Interpretation*
BJS	Brown Judaic Studies
BTB	*Biblical Theology Bulletin*
BZAW	Beihefte zur Zeitschrift für die alttestamentlische Wissenschaft
CBC	Cambridge Bible Commentary
CBQ	*Catholic Biblical Quarterly*
CBQMS	Catholic Biblical Quarterly Monograph Series
CC	Continental Commentaries
ConBOT	Coniectanea biblica: Old Testament Series
CTM	*Concordia Theological Monthly*
CurTM	*Currents in Theology and Mission*
ExpTim	*Expository Times*
FOTL	Forms of the Old Testament Literature

GBS	Guides to Biblical Study
HAR	*Hebrew Annual Review*
HUCA	*Hebrew Union College Annual*
IB	*Interpreter's Bible,* ed. George Arthur Buttrick et al. 12 vols. Nashville: Abingdon, 1951-57
ICC	International Critical Commentary
IDB	*The Interpreter's Dictionary of the Bible,* ed. George Arthur Buttrick. 4 vols. Nashville: Abingdon, 1962
Int	*Interpretation*
IRT	Issues in Religion and Theology
JAAR	*Journal of the American Academy of Religion*
JAOS	*Journal of the American Oriental Society*
JBL	*Journal of Biblical Literature*
JNES	*Journal of Near Eastern Studies*
JSOT	*Journal for the Study of the Old Testament*
JSOTSup	Journal for the Study of the Old Testament: Supplement Series
JSS	*Journal of Semitic Studies*
KJV	King James Version
NCBC	New Century Bible Commentary
NIDB	*New Interpreter's Dictionary of the Bible,* ed. Katharine Doob Sakenfeld. 5 vols. Nashville: Abingdon, 2009
NJPS	New Jewish Publication Society Version
NRSV	New Revised Standard Version
OBT	Overtures to Biblical Theology
OTL	Old Testament Library
PTMS	Pittsburgh Theological Monograph Series
RSV	Revised Standard Version
RTR	*Reformed Theological Review*
SBLMS	Society of Biblical Literature Monograph Series
SBT	Studies in Biblical Theology
SBTh	*Studia Biblica et Theologica*
SJOT	*Scandinavian Journal of the Old Testament*
SJT	*Scottish Journal of Theology*
TBC	Torch Bible Commentaries
TDNT	*Theological Dictionary of the New Testament,* ed. Gerhard Kittel and Gerhard Friedrich. 10 vols. Grand Rapids: Eerdmans, 1964-1976

TDOT	*Theological Dictionary of the Old Testament,* ed. G. Johannes Botterweck, Helmer Ringgren, and Heinz-Josef Fabry. Grand Rapids: Eerdmans, 1974–
TynBul	*Tyndale Bulletin*
VT	*Vetus Testamentum*
VTSup	Supplements to Vetus Testamentum
ZAW	*Zeitschrift für die alttestamentliche Wissenschaft*

Acknowledgment

Every time I write about wisdom books, and every time I teach Hebrew wisdom, I am again reminded of my debt to Professor James L. Crenshaw, my teacher and mentor at Vanderbilt University, who now teaches at Duke University.

Introduction

"You reap what you sow." "People get what they deserve." Do you agree? Is that the way you see the world? "Why do the righteous suffer?" "Why do bad things happen to good people?" How do you answer these questions? Do these issues ever trouble you? They deeply concerned the Hebrew sages. The sages argue that to be human, one must ultimately take a stand on whether or not life makes sense, whether or not human existence is organized according to some moral or rational order. The wisdom books of the Bible address all these issues, and the various sages answer the questions differently from the rest of the Hebrew Bible. They disagreed with each other as well.

The five wisdom books written by these sages fall into two distinct categories. The first we might call "Hebrew Wisdom." These are the books of Proverbs, Job, and Ecclesiastes. The second are "Greek Wisdom," Ben Sira and the Wisdom of Solomon. Hebrew Wisdom is distinguished from Greek Wisdom in manifold ways. First and most obviously, these three books are written in Hebrew, the other two, in Greek. But that is not exactly right, because Ben Sira had a Hebrew original, which had been lost for many centuries and then found early in the twentieth. One might distinguish these two classes of wisdom books chronologically. The first three books were written earlier than the second two. They were written before Alexander the Great conquered the territory of the Middle East and imposed Greek language and culture upon the region. This imposition, called Hellenism, transformed the Israelite wisdom tradition, and the last two books, Ben Sira and Wisdom of Solomon, show the effects.

The more important difference between the two classes of wisdom books is ideological and structured around their most deeply held beliefs. The first three books are more open. They freely expose their controversies and disagreements with each other. The authors of the second group mistrust outsiders and are defensive against strange ideas. The Hebrew Wisdom books avoid reference to the leading narratives of Israel. They know nothing of Abraham, Moses, David, or the Law. Where Solomon or David is mentioned, it is only to create the illusion that the great wise king, the son of David, wrote them. By contrast, the Greek Wisdom books refer copiously to the other parts of the Hebrew Bible.

Although they differ significantly, these books are not different species, nor do they come from entirely different worlds. Most everyone acknowledges these five as a distinct category among themselves and set apart from the other books of the Hebrew Bible. They are of a single type in many ways. They use similar vocabulary. The Greek Wisdom books, written later, show full awareness of many features from the earlier books. They pick up on most of the important themes found in Hebrew Wisdom, including the problem of innocent suffering and the distinction between the wise and the foolish. The book of Proverbs (Hebrew Wisdom) introduces the mysterious figure of "Woman Wisdom." Both Greek books then describe her in more detail. They draw from the book of Proverbs but reinterpret her.

The writers of all the wisdom books were thoroughly Yahwist. They regarded themselves as worshippers of the Israelite God whom they called Yahweh, and they believed that as sages they uncovered and interpreted the messages that Yahweh had embedded into the world. These messages, available to the carefully observant, only waited to be discovered.

The Hebrew Wisdom books feature a number of key characteristics. Even though Greek Wisdom (Ben Sira and Wisdom of Solomon) diverged from many of the following, these basic ideas remained part of their DNA, the building blocks with which they constructed their own contributions to the Israelite wisdom tradition.

The sages regarded the world of nature as a sacred text upon which Yahweh has written important insights about life. Sages disagree as to whether Yahweh's embedded message is easy or difficult to read. In either case, wisdom comes to those who carefully observe the ways of nature and the complexities of human behavior. From the ant they learn diligence. From the lazy farmer they learn the origin of famine and suffering. The sage learns principles from these observations, and by applying those principles, anyone may lead a good, happy, and successful life. Some sages asserted rather that God had placed wisdom too deep to be mined. The task of making sense of life then becomes impossible.

The wisdom literature was part of a teaching tradition. Any intellectual movement seeks to pass down its unique insights to the next generation. Second generation sages received the passed-on wisdom, but sometimes they rejected it and offered counterexplanations. This ongoing dialogue or debate too is part of the wisdom tradition. The wisdom books, taken together, are a field upon which a vast argument has taken place. The contemporary reader of ancient Israelite wisdom can eavesdrop upon the sages, but one is also forced to take part, to provide one's own answers to the deep and penetrating questions asked by the Israelite sages and their descendants.

Certain perennial problems gain the attention of the wisdom authors, who carry on the discussion through their books. First is the problem of evil, or innocent suffering. This issue is popularly framed by the question: "Why do bad things happen to good people?" The question assumes that a benevolent God governs the universe, and so innocent suffering ought not to happen. That the innocent do in fact suffer (obvious to almost everyone) suggested to the sages that God does not effectively govern creation, an inference they found disturbing. On the one hand, they were committed Yahwists who submitted to God as the sole governor of existence. On the other hand, their commitment to human observation as a genuine and important source of truth caused them to question their most basic assumptions about Yahweh. Was God too weak to address human concerns for justice and fairness? Did God care about human well-being? Each sage tried to solve this problem. Both of the Greek Wisdom books, Ben Sira and the Wisdom of Solomon, introduce new ways to understand the question, but they shape those ideas according to the older wisdom principles, and they seek to justify to a wisdom audience the changes they introduce.

This brings up another important issue. Although there were many pious sages who accepted the traditional understanding of God, many other parts of the Hebrew wisdom books (but not the Greek ones) express doubt and skepticism regarding God's goodness and reliability. This willingness to question goes hand in hand with the sages' commitment to observation. New evidence requires rethinking basic principles. The sages examined for flaws traditions they learned from earlier wisdom writings, and they also questioned the beliefs of the larger Israelite/Judean communities. For example, the early wisdom tradition passed on their belief in the reliability of the "law of retribution," that humans tend to get what they deserve. Then, the second generation sages noticed that evil people often got away with their crimes, while good and holy people would suffer pointlessly. Thus they came to doubt the law of retribution.[1] Such doubt and questioning become characteristic of late, Hebrew wisdom. However, such expressions of doubt should not be confused with unfaithfulness, or even sin. For the sage, doubt and questions were an integral part of the wisdom enterprise. Without raising questions, even some really fundamental questions, even some *painful* questions, one would never find the truth.

This volume addresses the following issues:

Chapter 1: Who Are the Sages?

The opening chapter examines the authorship of the wisdom books, focusing mostly on Hebrew Wisdom (Job, Proverbs, and Ecclesiastes). Greek Wisdom authorship is covered subsequently. The critical problem concerns the identification of the authors. It will be much easier to identify and describe those who wrote the two Greek books. However, the authors of Proverbs, Job, and Ecclesiastes actively conceal their identity. Chapter 1 reveals them as the professional guild of intellectuals who taught the upper classes and served as advisors and bureaucrats to royalty and as diplomats. Tribal and village wisdom, still reflected in some of the earlier proverbs, consists of informal teaching from parents and elders in the communities.

Chapter 2: What Unity in Proverbs?

The book of Proverbs brings together a large group of pithy phrases and extended poems, calling all of them proverbs (Hebrew *mashal*). It is a collection of collections, extraordinarily diverse. Two themes dominate the book. The first consists of an argument between sages. They disagree regarding what is the best way to gain wisdom. Some favored a human-centered approach based on observation. Others opted for a pious trust in

---

1. David Penchansky, "Divine Retribution," in *NIDB*, 2.

God's unfathomable mystery. In the second major theme, the author introduces and describes Woman Wisdom (Hebrew *Hokmah*), the most compelling character featured in biblical wisdom. She and her counterpart, the strange or foreign woman, struggle to gain converts and disciples among the young students in Israel. In this chapter I try (and fail) to bring together these two themes into a single coherent message.

Chapter 3: The Meaning of the Book of Job

What happens when a perfectly righteous person, for no apparent reason, suffers the loss of family, home, and finally his health? This book raises questions about God's goodness, and even his competence. Although Job at the end lives "happily ever after," there is much that undermines this neat ending.

Chapter 4: Wisdom, Madness, and Folly: The Three Qoheleths

Qoheleth is the title or name in Hebrew of the author of the book of Ecclesiastes. It means something like "public teacher," or "speaker." Three distinct and ultimately incompatible positions stalk the pages of this enigmatic book. As a result, Qoheleth questions virtually every major religious claim found elsewhere in the Bible. The author asks whether wisdom is better than folly, life better than death. Everything turns joyless in the face of its inevitable end. Ecclesiastes has some of the most depressing and seditious sentiments found anywhere in the Hebrew Scripture.

Chapter 5: Sounds of Silence: The *Absence* of Covenantal Theology in the Wisdom Literature

This chapter examines a feature found in the first three wisdom books, which I must address before going on to Greek Wisdom. These three Hebrew Wisdom books are unique because they do not refer to Israelite sacred history, specifically common biblical themes such as the covenants with Abraham, Moses, and David. Further, there is no mention of Israelite history, kings, or prophets. In this chapter I try to imagine a community of sages in Israel that would not mention these stories, stories they must have known. There are a few possible solutions to this mystery.

Chapter 6: Sophia and Simon: The Two Poles of Ben Sira's Affection

Two images dominate the Greek Wisdom book of Ben Sira.[2] They are Sophia, the goddess of wisdom, and Simon, the high priest of Israel, who at the time of writing had recently died. How do these two fit together? Also, in this book the author for the first time among the sages refers to the Israelite narratives that had been ignored by his earlier colleagues. Finally, in his most dramatic contribution to the wisdom tradition, Ben Sira equates Woman Wisdom with Torah, the biblical law ascribed to Moses.

Chapter 7: The Conservatism of Pseudo-Solomon

The author of the Wisdom of Solomon introduces a radical change to Israelite consciousness. He is the first sage, and one of the first biblical writers, to suggest that the problem of innocent suffering would be solved by the existence of a grand accounting by God after an individual's death. Previous to this, Israelite writers were vague and agnostic about what happens to individuals after they die. Things might not be fair at the end of this life, Pseudo-Solomon says, but in the afterlife the good will be rewarded for their suffering, while all the wicked will be punished.

This book's subtitle, "Conflict and Dissonance," employs two metaphors to characterize wisdom books. I will now expand upon these two metaphors, and then suggest a few others to round out my point. If I included them all, it would have made the title unmanageable.

This is what I mean by "conflict" — that the sages take strong, adversarial positions against the writers of other wisdom books, and perhaps even stronger adversarial positions against different political and religious groups in Israel. The sages fight with each other and against everybody else. There are strong, substantive disagreements between the warring parties, and much is at stake. The sages were neither passive nor tolerant in their debate. Conflict is a combat metaphor. It brings to mind a war, a fight, or a clash of wills.

2. This book has other names: Sirach, Ecclesiasticus, and the Wisdom of Jesus Ben Sira.

The wisdom books are a site of conflict. The sages disagreed with each other, and they disagreed with the larger Israelite society. These disagreements produced conflict, hostility, and strong opposition. They wrote about their conflicts. Sometimes they appended their disagreements as part of an older work, making sure to get their word in, so that their voice would be heard by future generations. Sometimes they penned whole new works responding to an older, discredited position.

"Dissonance" refers to a clash of sounds that irritates the ear. A harmonic text would read smoothly, with no apparent contradictions or obvious seams. A dissonant text has disparate parts that cannot easily be fitted together. At the same time, subsequent readers will want to smooth out the text, or better, to prove that the text, properly understood, was harmonious all along.

The wisdom books of the Bible have often been subject to this kind of treatment. Individual books have been made to speak with a single voice — the wisdom books as a whole agree with each other, and fit in with the other parts of the Hebrew Bible. I suppose that readers do that because they believe that the Bible, being a holy book, must never have contradictions.

But as any musician or composer will tell you, dissonance is a vital part of a musical piece, and some of the greatest musical compositions show new ways to understand dissonant sounds. Therefore, by ignoring the dissonance or smoothing it over, the interpreter misses the finest moments in Hebrew wisdom.

Here are some other useful metaphors for the wisdom literature of the Bible, metaphors not included in the title: "Contradiction" is a more general way to understand the clash of ideas in the wisdom books, using a logical or philosophical metaphor. Some sages make assertions that directly contradict a different sage's earlier stated position. Sometimes these conflicting ideas are put into the mouths of characters in narratives (in the book of Job, for instance). Sometimes these arguments are patched together in a single book (Ecclesiastes, for instance); sometimes a later book challenges ideas put forth in earlier books (as Wisdom of Solomon challenges Ecclesiastes). And further, in many ways implicit and explicit, the sages stood against some better organized nonwisdom groups in Israel, such as the prophetic guilds and the priests. Each group saw themselves as defenders of the Israelite tradition.

I have my own opinion as to which wisdom "schools" are truly wise, and which mindlessly parrot what their masters (those who pay them) want them to say. However, of much greater interest are *the contradictions themselves.* I pay attention to these "fissures" (using a geological metaphor) as the key to a text's meaning. Although I suspect that this is true with all sacred literature, I am certain that it is characteristic of the body of wisdom material in the Bible — that the contradictions in the text are those features that produce the meaning.[3]

For example, the author of Proverbs enjoins readers to trust completely in Yahweh. The book of Job suggests (as we shall see) that God might not be worthy of that trust. This is an instance of one sage disputing what another says. In addition, many conflicts take place between the wisdom tradition and the other, more well-known biblical traditions, those from the priestly guilds or the prophets, for instance. The disparity between the wisdom tradition and the rest of the Bible is the subject of Chapter 1 and also Chapter 5.

Wisdom literature is full of these clashings. One finds a dramatic example in Prov 26:4-5:

Do not answer fools according to their folly,
or you will be a fool yourself.
Answer fools according to their folly,
or they will be wise in their own eyes.

Many aspects of wisdom conflict with fundamental ideas found in the rest of the Hebrew Bible. I will look for these places, and examine them, but not for purposes of "solving" the conflict. I will not attempt to show how they do not *really* conflict if read correctly. Rather, I will examine these places in the wisdom texts to demonstrate how meaning is produced at the site of contradiction, like the eruptions produced by the grinding of tectonic plates or the sparks produced by flint and iron. Wisdom then is not about boiling down the various books into a few summative positions, but rather about exploring and elucidating the contours of the fault lines in the text and seeing how they take hold.

To get at those conflicts, my especial attention will be upon the literary features of a text. These features are the constituents of any work of litera-

3. I explore this theory more fully in the first chapter of *The Betrayal of God* (Louisville: Westminster John Knox, 1990) and in the book *The Politics of Biblical Theology* (Macon: Mercer University Press, 1995).

ture, elements such as character, plot, and theme. Throughout this book, although I will not draw attention to my literary approach, I will ask literary-type questions of the text, such as whose voice narrates the text and who is its expected audience. If the text is a story, or a part of the story, I will look for its climax, when all the forces of the story come together in a great resolution. I will ask regarding the characters in every wisdom book, what are they like? Do they change?

Why should we care about this literature, these five books? They are worthy of our attention because the questions that they ask are human questions, ones that emerge from the depths of people's experience. Many wonder at the meaning of existence, the possibility for happiness, the inevitability of death. The sages address these terrifying questions fearlessly. They stare boldly into the abyss, the darkness that surrounds us. Their voices provide a guide of how to navigate through life. The sages tend to approach these questions in a practical, down-to-earth manner. They trust their own observations and judgments. They seek to learn from other cultures. They do not limit themselves to purely Israelite ideas. Our world contains many cultures with linked destinies. The authors of these books have learned to live with the ambiguity of different points of view side by side. In a world where too many expressions of religion are intolerant of difference, the sages' exposure to different ideas made them stronger.

Finally, these books have value because they question the most sacred assumptions of the Israelite religion. For the sages, raising questions is a sacred duty, and doubt becomes holy. They have a divine obligation to question the claims of those in authority, and to reexamine widely held religious ideas. In contemporary time, people likewise must question the authorities and point out their mistakes and lies. Biblical wisdom literature shows us a way.

Except where indicated, I will use the New Revised Standard Version for quotations from the Bible. The NRSV translators used LORD to translate Yahweh, the divine name of the God of Israel. This name Yahweh was used to distinguish Israel's God from the gods of other nations. In this book I will often use the term Yahweh to indicate that it is a personal name and not a generic description.

QUESTIONS FOR REVIEW

Q What are the differences between Hebrew wisdom and Hellenistic wisdom? What are the similarities?

Q Why are both Hebrew and Greek wisdom considered the same type of literature?

Q In what way is wisdom literature part of a teaching tradition?

Q What is the problem of evil, and why is it a problem?

Q What is the role of doubt and questioning in the wisdom tradition?

Q Why does the author say that the biblical wisdom books are worthy of our attention?

KEY WORDS

– Sage

– Hellenism

– Alexander the Great

FOR FURTHER READING

Crenshaw, James L. *Old Testament Wisdom: An Introduction.* Atlanta: John Knox, 1981; 3rd ed., Louisville: Westminster John Knox, 2010.

1. Who Are the Sages?

Now the serpent was more crafty than any other wild animal that the Lord *God had made.*

GENESIS 3:1

"But my lord has wisdom like the wisdom of the angel of God to know all things that are on the earth."

2 SAMUEL 14:20

The sage, or wizard, takes prominent place in the stories of many cultures. From Merlin, Gandalf, and Dumbledore in the Anglo-American tradition to the placid Zen monks who lived in Japanese villages, there have been individuals with a deeper understanding of things, people who give advice. They knew how things worked and the right thing to do.

Wisdom begins in the family, in the villages and tribes. This happens three ways. First, parents share their wisdom and experience with children. Second, older people in the community serve as a source of wisdom to the younger generations. Finally, the villagers regard certain individuals within their community as wise, and a source of good judgment. People go to them with problems, disputes, and questions. Among the wisdom books, certain parts of the book of Proverbs reflect these early forms of wisdom. This localized, informal wisdom activity continued throughout

Israel's history, but except for the book of Proverbs, no one preserved their insights in written form.[1]

During the Israelite monarchy there emerged a professional sage class. Many biblical wisdom scholars question this, but the circumstantial evidence supports their existence. This professional class wrote and edited early forms of the books of Proverbs, Job, and Ecclesiastes. The authors of these wisdom books were sages, "the wise," who served as the "wizards" of ancient Israel. They wrote the wisdom books during a period that spanned no more than a few hundred years. It should have been relatively easy to examine these works and determine who wrote them, why, and what was happening at the time. It *should* be easy, but it is not. The authors of the first three wisdom books deliberately concealed their identity.

Why would these authors not want people to know who they were? Perhaps the sages thought that by avoiding specific references to their identity and time of writing, they demonstrated the more universal nature of their work. They did not intend their writing for Israel only. It was meant for all peoples and for all time. It was not meant for *Israel* in particular, so the first three books scarcely give a hint of the authors' own national identity. For example, Job was an Edomite (from a land due south of Israel), and from even further south, in Egypt, the Israelite sages freely borrowed Egyptian proverbs for their collections.

This makes it difficult to determine the identity and nature of these authors. Therefore, one finds out more about the characteristics of the sages, "the wise," by looking at things written about them, rather than what they wrote themselves. The group responsible for the wisdom books made its presence felt in other Israelite literature of the same period. The following features in nonwisdom books suggest the presence of a wisdom ideology: use of wisdom vocabulary; reference to individuals known as "the wise" (Heb. *ḥakam*); individuals who give advice, wisdom, or counsel to kings; narratives where characters stand out as especially wise; or members of a guild who are initiate in secret wisdom, such as magicians.

There are two different, broad ways that scholars have regarded the

---

1. A few proverblike lines appear in certain other biblical narratives. In Judges, for instance, Samson says: "What is sweeter than honey? What is stronger than a lion?" (Judg 14:18). Such proverbs are evidence of village wisdom.

presence of "wisdom" perspective in the rest of the Bible. Some claim that the sages influenced the composition of many biblical books. An alternate approach claims that individuals who wrote the wisdom books were not "the wise," but rather were part of a broad intellectual movement, not a wisdom "class" but an intellectual tradition.[2] Whether these wisdom books were written by "the wise" or by otherwise employed, educated Israelites, wisdom and wisdom influence were to be found in many parts of the Bible. For instance, British scholar Norman Whybray wrote about wisdom influence in the David story (1 Samuel 16–1 Kings 1).[3] Because the narrative dealt in morally ambiguous ways with a whole host of situations, he claimed it would be especially useful for the instruction of scribes. Eager young students who read the courtly advice in Proverbs would consult these novelistic treatments about Joseph and David (now in Genesis and 2 Samuel), which functioned as "case studies." Whybray and others believe that wisdom tradition is the invisible hand that formed much of the Hebrew Bible. After Whybray, scholars began to see wisdom influence in many places in the Bible. They claimed that wisdom perspective pervades the whole of the Hebrew canon, noting, for instance, proverblike language in the prophets. For instance, in both Proverbs and Amos we find the same type of numerical proverb:

> The leech has two daughters;
> "Give, give," they cry.
> *Three* things are never satisfied;
> *four* never say, "Enough." (Prov 30:15)

Similarly in Amos one reads:

> Thus says the LORD:
> For *three* transgressions of Israel,
> and for *four*, I will not revoke the punishment;
> because they sell the righteous for silver,
> and the needy for a pair of sandals. (Amos 2:6)

---

2. R. N. Whybray, *The Intellectual Tradition in the Old Testament* (BZAW 135; Berlin: de Gruyter, 1974).

3. R. N. Whybray, *The Succession Narrative: A Study of II Samuel 9-20; I Kings 1 and 2* (SBT, 2nd ser. 9; Naperville: Allenson, 1968).

These wisdom scholars find in the Joseph story in Genesis an exemplary tale of a courtly sage:

> So Pharaoh said to Joseph, "Since God has shown you all this, there is no one so discerning and wise as you. You shall be over my house, and all my people shall order themselves as you command. (Gen 41:39-40)

In the story of David, wise counselors appear at moments of crisis in both David's political and family dramas. (I examine them in detail below.)

Both the books of Proverbs and Job contain accounts of the creation of the universe. In Job it says:

> "Where were you when I laid the foundation of the earth?
> Tell me, if you have understanding.
> Who determined its measurements . . .
> when the morning stars sang together
> and all the heavenly beings shouted for joy?" (Job 38:4-7)

In Proverbs, Woman Wisdom speaks:

> When there were no depths I was brought forth,
> when there were no springs abounding with water.
> Before the mountains had been shaped,
> . . . When he established the heavens, I was there. . . . (Prov 8:24-28)

That draws attention to Genesis:

> . . . the earth was a formless void and darkness covered the face of the deep, while a wind from God swept over the face of the waters. (Gen 1:2)

Perhaps then both the sages (who wrote Proverbs and Job) and the author of Genesis 1 drew from the same source and were part of the same group. The approach of Whybray and others to understanding the sages in other parts of the Bible claims that wisdom had a strong and positive presence in the Bible.

James Crenshaw demonstrated the deficiencies of this suggestion. He examined many of the examples of so-called "wisdom influence" and found them unconvincing. He asserted that many of the "wisdom words" found outside of the wisdom books have a common usage throughout the Israelite culture, and their presence alone does not necessarily suggest authorship by a wisdom group.[4]

Rather than seeing the rest of the Bible as wisdom-shaped, the second approach to understanding the sages is quite the opposite. It notes instead that many biblical authors regarded "the wise" with disdain and hostility. If this is the case (and I think it is), then we have a treasure trove of testimony as to the role and function of "the wise" in ancient Israel. That it comes from those who thought the wise a bad influence on the Israelite youth makes it that much more interesting to examine first. One learns most from those who are not prone to flattery.

The following are biblical passages that suggest (a) the existence of a group of sages and (b) that they are regarded as a negative or questionable influence in ancient Israel.

The first sage in the Bible is the serpent who speaks to Eve in the garden of Eden.[5] The serpent is not Satan, or the devil, although Christians and Muslims have commonly interpreted the story this way. Rather, the text of Genesis says that the serpent is a "wild animal that the LORD God made" (Gen 3:1). Why would the writer take pains to make this point about the serpent, unless to argue against someone who might have claimed the opposite, that the serpent is a divine or supernatural being? The writer of Genesis 2–3 insists that the serpent is not a supernatural being, but rather one of the animals.

However, this animal talks and seems to be intelligent. The writer explains this by describing the serpent as crafty. "Crafty" (Heb. *'arum*) is a word with many shades of meaning. The Hebrew word has a very similar import to the English word "crafty." Both may mean sneaky, underhanded, or deceptive, but also skillful, competent, and even wise. The serpent is just a beast, but a particularly wise one. And just like a sage advising a king, the serpent gives advice to the first humans. The depiction of the serpent in Genesis reflects upon sages who advise kings, and who claim special insight into the ways things work in the world.

This garden of Eden story that the Israelites told reflected their ambig-

---

4. See, e.g., James L. Crenshaw, "The Influence of the Wise upon Amos: The 'Doxologies of Amos' and Job 5,9-16; 9,5-10," *ZAW* 79 (1967): 42-52; and "Method in Determining Wisdom Influence upon 'Historical' Literature," *JBL* 88 (1969): 129-42.

5. The garden of Eden story (Genesis 2–3) is not the oldest writing in the Bible, but is likely quite early.

uous relationship with the wisdom tradition and to the sages. Yahweh had said that the tree would kill them. The serpent told the woman that contrary to what Yahweh had said, the tree of the knowledge of good and evil would not kill them. Rather, they would become wise like Yahweh, and that was the reason Yahweh did not want them to eat from it. Surprisingly, the serpent told only truth to the first woman. They did not die. Eating the fruit of the tree of the knowledge of good and evil *did* open their eyes, and they *did* become like God, knowing good and evil.[6] So the wise counselor had given sage advice. He told them, "Do not listen to Yahweh, but instead use your own senses and reasoning to make an intelligent decision." However, the first humans felt shame after eating the fruit and accused each other. Harmony was broken. They proved incapable of clothing themselves. They used leaves. Yahweh clothed them properly with animal skins. The serpent did not warn them of these negative consequences. The writer of this story suspected that wisdom, or counsel from the wise, might lead to harm.

In another example, Amnon, the oldest son of King David, wants his half-sister Tamar in marriage. Such a union seems forbidden to him, and he is sick with desire for her. Only when a cousin and friend, Jonadab, gives him advice does he get what he wanted. Jonadab is described by the narrator as "a very wise person" (2 Sam 13:3-5) (Heb. ḥakam me'od).[7] The advice he gives enables Amnon to seduce and rape the young Tamar. That is not a very satisfactory endorsement of ḥakam. Subsequently, Absalom, Tamar's full brother, murders Amnon, and David banishes his surviving son from Jerusalem.

Next, Joab, King David's military commander, hires an unnamed wise woman (Heb. 'ishsha ḥakamah) of Tekoa to convince the king to absolve the murderer of Amnon and lift his banishment. Through her flattery of the king ("But my lord has wisdom [Heb. ḥakam] like the wisdom of the angel of God to know all things that are on the earth" [2 Sam 14:20]), she persuades him to lift the banishment. Absalom returns and subsequently organizes a rebellion against the king so that David had to flee his capital and run to save his life. One of David's counselors (Heb. yo'ets, another wisdom word), Ahithophel joins the rebellion against his former em-

---

6. See chapter 1 of my *What Rough Beast: Images of God in the Hebrew Bible* (Louisville: Westminster John Knox, 1999) for a full treatment of the garden of Eden story.

7. The NRSV translates "a very crafty man."

ployer. Ahithophel advises Absalom to march against David while the king's army is weary and in retreat, but a spy planted by David gives "better advice." When Ahithophel sees that his counsel (Heb. *'etsah*) is not taken and that Absalom's army is destroyed, the sage commits suicide (2 Samuel 15–17).

The prophets First Isaiah (eighth century) and Jeremiah (sixth century) strongly criticize the *ḥakam*. The Israelite prophets and the sages had a long-standing feud based on their fundamentally different orientations. The prophets received their information as direct revelation from God. The sages believed their messages came from their own careful observation and power to reason. The prophets were nationalists and believed their nation destined to dominate and rule the other nations. The sages were more open to other cultures, particularly those that had a long wisdom tradition like their own. Proverbs 22:17–24:22 are copied and adapted from the Egyptian Instructions of Amenhotep. This was acceptable practice when Egypt was an ally of Judah, but when the pharaoh became an enemy, the prophets questioned the sages' loyalty. Isaiah says:

> Alas for those who go down to Egypt for help
> and who rely on horses,
> who trust in chariots because they are many
> and in horsemen because they are very strong,
> but do not look to the Holy One of Israel
> or consult the LORD!
> Yet he too is wise and brings disaster. (Isa 31:1-2)

"He too is wise." That statement drips with contempt for the people who claim to have a reliable source of wisdom or identify themselves as *the* wise. Yahweh too is wise, Isaiah says, and he will see to their destruction.

> Oh, rebellious children, says the LORD,
> who carry out a plan (Heb. *'etsah*), but not mine;
> who make an alliance, but against my will,
> adding sin to sin;
> who set out to go down to Egypt
> without asking for my counsel,
> to take refuge in the protection of Pharaoh,
> and to seek shelter in the shadow of Egypt. (Isa 30:1-2)

The key word is "plan," spoken ironically, addressed to those who ordinarily give counsel, like Ahithophel. Isaiah accuses them of making plans against Yahweh's will.

Jeremiah says,

> The wise *(ḥakamim)* shall be put to shame,
> they shall be dismayed and taken;
> since they have rejected the word of the LORD,
> what wisdom is in them? (Jer 8:9)

In what way did they "reject Yahweh's word"? There was a live political debate taking place in the courts of the king of Judah (as there was in every other petty kingdom in that region) about whether to seek an alliance with one of the other superpowers against the burgeoning threat of Babylon. From Jeremiah's perspective, the tide was turning, and one should join one's fortunes to the Babylonian emperor. The sages took the opposite approach, advising a strategic alliance with the Egyptians. For Jeremiah, that constituted "rejecting Yahweh's word."

In both First Isaiah and Jeremiah, widely apart in time, the prophet attacks a group of people called the wise, who give counsel to kings and who support a strategic alliance against a northern threat. In the case of First Isaiah, the threat was from the Assyrians, and in the case of Jeremiah, the Babylonians. The fact that neither prophet likes or approves of "the wise" is not an argument against their existence. The attitude of these prophets fits nicely with the depiction of the wise in the other stories we have cited. They suggest that at the time of their writing a group of the wise struggled against certain prophets regarding the proper foreign policy towards the superpowers in a time of struggle and transition.

There is only one positive portrayal of a sagelike figure in the Hebrew Bible. In Egypt, in the story of Joseph (Genesis 37-50), Joseph's skills compete with the wisdom of the court magicians.[8] The narrator describes Joseph's adversaries collectively as "the wise ones and the sorcerers/magi-

---

8. Compare with Moses' confrontation with Egyptian magicians in Exod 7:11: "Then Pharaoh summoned the wise men (Heb. *ḥakamim*) and the sorcerers; and they also, the magicians of Egypt, did the same by their secret arts." This is similar to Genesis: "In the morning his spirit was troubled; so he sent and called for all the magicians of Egypt and all its wise men (Heb. *ḥakamim*)" (Gen 41:8). In both cases, the group called "the wise" *opposes* the protagonist, Joseph or Moses.

cians." However, the narrator specifies that Joseph gets his wisdom from God and not from observation or wisdom tradition. "And Joseph said to them, 'Do not interpretations belong to God?'" (Gen 40:8); "'It is not I; God will give Pharaoh a favorable answer'" (Gen 41:16).

Whereas the wise and the magicians are unable to interpret the Pharaoh's dreams, the Hebrew prisoner Joseph can. Does that make Joseph a superior wizard? Wisdom scholars argue: Is the Joseph story in the Bible a paradigmatic wisdom tale, and is Joseph the ideal wise courtier? Whybray suggests that the story of Joseph was used as a textbook in wisdom schools, in order to teach young men how to serve as effective courtiers to the king. Joseph advises the king, and his advice is wise. Joseph saves the kingdom from a terrible famine, enriches the Pharaoh, and strengthens his authority.

Joseph is expert at interpreting dreams, but it is not his wisdom that enables him to see their meaning. Rather, Yahweh reveals the meaning of the Pharaoh's dream. This is more the way a prophet receives messages from God. If Joseph acted like a sage he would say, "I will figure out the dreams based on my experience interpreting other people's dreams, and because I have been initiated into a guild of people who interpret dreams." Joseph says, rather, "Do not interpretations belong to God?" He appears more a prophet than a sage.

The evidence is circumstantial, but strong, that the sages described by the storytellers and prophets mentioned above are the authors of the wisdom books. The vocabulary of the wisdom books includes the same words used to describe the sages in the nonwisdom books, words such as "wisdom," "knowledge," "understanding," "insight," and "counsel." For instance, the author of Proverbs describes that books should be used:

> For learning about wisdom and instruction,
> for understanding words of insight,
> for gaining instruction in wise dealing,
> righteousness, justice, and equity;
> to teach shrewdness to the simple,
> knowledge and prudence to the young —
> Let the wise also hear and gain in learning,
> and the discerning acquire skill,
> to understand a proverb and a figure,
> the words of the wise and their riddles. (Prov 1:2-6)

If we make this crucial connection between the figures called "the wise," who give advice to kings, and the authors of the first three wisdom books, we can make the following conclusions. First, the tradition of wisdom which began informally through family and tribal relationships, in the urban centers developed as a professional guild. This began at least from the time of Isaiah's Assyrian crisis, but perhaps a good deal earlier. Second, these sages often came into conflict with other religious groups within Israel. They based their conflict upon different sources of information and different interpretations of international affairs. The sages were regarded by many of their peers as irreligious, lacking national loyalty, arrogant, trusting in their own insights rather than supernatural revelation. The prophets accused them of trusting in their own wisdom rather than trusting in Yahweh. The challenges were mostly unfair, but they indicated that the sages, the wisdom enterprise, and the wisdom books threatened the core beliefs of other powerful organizations and individuals in Israel.

QUESTIONS FOR REVIEW

Q What is the nature of village wisdom?

Q Why did the Hebrew sages conceal their identity?

Q Some say the sages greatly influenced the other parts of the Bible. What evidence supports this argument?

Q Others say that the sages were an unpopular minority. What evidence supports this argument? Which argument do you find more persuasive?

Q In what way is the serpent in the garden of Eden a sage?

KEY WORDS

– Crafty

– Tree of the knowledge of good and evil

– Amnon, Jonadab, Tamar

– First Isaiah and Jeremiah

– Egypt

FOR FURTHER READING

Crenshaw, James L. "Method in Determining Wisdom Influence upon 'Historical' Literature." *JBL* 88 (1969): 129-42.
Penchansky, David. *What Rough Beast: Images of God in the Hebrew Bible.* Louisville: Westminster John Knox, 1999, chapter 1.
Whybray, R. N. *The Intellectual Tradition in Israel.* BZAW 135. Berlin: de Gruyter, 1974.
————. *The Succession Narrative: A Study of II Samuel 9-20; I Kings 1 and 2.* SBT, 2nd ser. 9. Naperville: Allenson, 1968.

2. What Unity in Proverbs?

The fear of Yahweh is the beginning of knowledge.

PROVERBS 1:7

The beginning of wisdom is this: Get wisdom.

PROVERBS 4:7

Some years ago, when I began to write this introduction to the wisdom literature of the Bible, I saved the book of Proverbs for last. I knew it would be difficult to say anything about a book that has no real structure, with no distinctive style or perspective. This makes it tricky to make meaningful comments about the book as a whole. Nevertheless, in this chapter I will try to do that.

I explore here two important themes that go some way towards getting at a sense of the entire book. The first regards a dispute between two groups of sages as to the nature of wisdom. The second regards the figure of Hokmah, Woman Wisdom.

The Dispute between the "Fear God" Sages and the "Get Wisdom" Sages

If we presume that there is a community of sages, intellectuals, who wrote the wisdom books of the Bible, there would be (as one would expect) disagreements on key issues. In Proverbs, a major controversy regards two distinct perspectives on what it means to be wise. One I call the "Fear Yahweh" group. They believe that the wisdom enterprise begins by fearing Yahweh. "The fear of Yahweh is the beginning of knowledge," they say (1:7). "Fearing Yahweh" is a difficult phrase to define — it means both everything and nothing. It has the sense of servile, abject terror in the face of a massively superior and hostile heavenly being, or it might connote "piety," "religiously precise behavior." By either definition, those who fear God expect God's power to overrule human plans and expectations.

The other perspective I call the "Get Wisdom" group. They believe that wisdom comprises careful observation of nature and human behavior, and by means of that observation they discern the best way to behave so as to assure success. Wisdom, they say, begins by "getting wisdom," that is, with their own observations and judgments, constantly tested by subsequent experience. These sages have figured out the way the universe works. But the "Fear Yahweh" sages believe that the ways of the Almighty remain a closed book to the human community, and one can only respond by "fearing God." God's ways are too mysterious to be explained in a straightforward manner, they say, and in fact one never knows what God will do. God enjoys destroying human plans and intentions.[1]

The "Get Wisdom" group believes that God (or the universe) reliably and consistently enforces the rules, that good deeds and wise decisions are always rewarded and bad deeds punished, to an exact corresponding degree, and that all this takes place in the present life. These sages sought to determine the mechanisms by which God governs the world, so that by means of that knowledge they could accurately predict how God might act in a given situation and make the appropriate choices.

The two groups share basic assumptions. They both believe that Yahweh is the source of all wisdom, is the great and powerful God, and they worship Yahweh. Additionally, they are optimistic and conservative — optimistic in that they believe that a just and fair God governs the universe; conservative, in that each acknowledges the authority of the elders

---

1. Some have suggested the debate is between those who claim that the universe itself enforces the rules through natural consequence and those who argue that God more directly brings the consequences. This is the wrong question. I agree with Gerhard von Rad that even when not explicit, the entirety of wisdom is pervaded by an intense Yahwism. *Old Testament Theology*, 1 (New York: Harper & Row, 1962), 60. There are no secular proverbs, nor any event not caused by the gods.

(parents or teachers) and emphasizes the importance of the tradition that they handed down.

The sages ask whether it is possible to know how to live. The "Get Wisdom" group says yes, through careful observation of both the natural world and the human community. The "Fear Yahweh" group says no, God overrules human plans and human insight, and ultimately wisdom cannot be found, but is clouded in deep mystery. Gerhard von Rad and others have tried to reconcile these two sides, saying that the "Get Wisdom" crowd was always aware of their limitations. They believed that one could get wisdom, but that wisdom was always limited. What von Rad fails to note, however, is that the confidence represented by some of the "Get Wisdom" proverbs conflicts irreparably with notions of divine inscrutability.[2] For example:

> For the upright will abide in the land,
> and the innocent will remain in it;
> but the wicked will be cut off from the land,
> and the treacherous will be rooted out of it. (Prov 2:21-22)

"Get Wisdom" claims that what can be known of God is sufficient to accommodate one's life and assure oneself success. The "Fear Yahweh" group claims that God intervenes in inexplicable ways. One cannot be sure of success, or of anything, for that matter. Therefore one should fear Yahweh. Consider this passage from Proverbs 3:

> Trust in Yahweh with all your heart,
> and do not rely on your own insight. . . .
> Do not be wise in your own eyes;
> fear Yahweh, and turn away from evil. (Prov 3:5, 7)

One might interpret this "don't be overly proud," an exhortation to humility. But I rather think it means "don't think that you have things figured out, that you can discern the secret for success."

---

2. James L. Crenshaw, "The Concept of God in Old Testament Wisdom," in *In Search of Wisdom: Essays in Memory of John G. Gammie*, ed. Leo G. Purdue, Bernard Brandon Scott, and William Johnston Wiseman (Louisville: Westminster John Knox, 1993), 6-7; William McKane, *Prophets and Wise Men* (SBT, 2nd ser. 44; Naperville: Allenson, 1965), 50-51, 53.

The "Get Wisdom" writer responds like this: "The beginning of wisdom is this: Get wisdom" (4:7). The "Fear Yahweh" sage says one should begin with the "fear of Yahweh." The "Get Wisdom" sage says that one must begin by "getting wisdom." The "Get Wisdom" group refuses to look beyond human wisdom to something contrary to it and superior. They reject the fear of Yahweh as the ground of all successful human behavior. Rather, they say, God created and placed patterns in existence and it behooves the sage to begin and end the quest with wisdom, which is nothing more than seeing those patterns and acting on their basis to achieve success.

Proverbs represents these two competing but both very *conventional* approaches to the wisdom tradition. This should not surprise, as they are the earliest of the Israelite wisdom writings. Unlike Job and Qoheleth, the writers of Proverbs for the most part neither challenge the status quo nor attack the justice of God. R. B. Y. Scott suggests that (except for Proverbs 8 and 30) the individual verses tend to be optimistic and conservative, consisting of "brief rhythmic adages and maxims."

These two wisdom philosophies began as a response to the problem of evil. They sought to explain why bad things happen to good people. The "Fear Yahweh" group says that we cannot know the ways of God but must respond by fearing. The "Get Wisdom" group says that if we obey the principles built into the universe, we will succeed. Disaster comes upon the foolish. They claim that one avoids evil through wise behavior. People suffer because they are not wise. The other group ("Fear Yahweh") believes that the fundamental principles built into the universe by Yahweh are not accessible to human discovery. Therefore, one can do all the right things to achieve success, but Yahweh, acting freely, unconstrained by any human plan or devising, can intervene and shatter human plans.[3] For instance, it says:

The human mind plans the way,
but Yahweh directs the steps. (16:9)

3. R. B. Y. Scott, *Proverbs. Ecclesiastes* (AB 18; Garden City: Doubleday, 1965), 23. There is in Scott a tensive description of the sages. First are those who depend upon themselves and their own perception to reach reality, which they presumably identify with how God created the world. Second are those who see the world shrouded in deep mystery and for whom any wisdom, any goodness, comes as a gift from this inscrutable God. Scott sees these as representing ideologies behind different parts of the collection — the more secular being earlier (folk and early monarchic) and the more religious being later.

All our steps are ordered by Yahweh;
how then can we understand our own ways? (20:24)[4]

Only in chapter 30 do we get anyone who questions the basic assumptions shared by both the "Fear God" and "Get Wisdom" groups.[5] The otherwise unknown Agur laments with cynical fatigue:

Thus says the man:

I am weary, O God,
    I am weary, O God. How can I prevail?
Surely I am too stupid to be human;
    I do not have human understanding.
I have not learned wisdom,
    nor have I knowledge of the holy ones. (30:1-3)

The passage is introduced, "thus says the man . . .," in stark contrast to the prophetic formula, "thus says Yahweh." This passage proves extraordinarily difficult to translate, let alone interpret. At very least this is one who despairs of the wisdom project altogether, not one who has figured things out, nor one who would exhort his readers to "fear Yahweh."[6]

These two groups were mocked mercilessly in the book of Job, where the hapless friends take the various positions — these very same positions — that one finds fresh and unironically presented in Proverbs. Zophar, one of Job's friends, speaks in a manner similar to the "Fear Yahweh" group:

Can you find out the deep things of God?
Can you find out the limit of the Almighty?

---

4. See also: "The plans of the mind belong to mortals,/but the answer of the tongue is from the LORD" (16:1); "The lot is cast into the lap,/but the decision is the LORD's alone" (16:33); "The horse is made ready for the day of battle,/but the victory belongs to the LORD" (21:31).

5. Assumption 1: that God is just and fairly and effectively governs the universe. Assumption 2: that the elders knew the right way to live and they have passed that wisdom on to us in the form of Proverbs.

6. James L. Crenshaw suggests that Agur here goes beyond the skepticism of Qoheleth into a raw cynicism, the strongest in the Bible; *Old Testament Wisdom* (Atlanta: John Knox, 1981), 194.

It is higher than heaven — what can you do?
Deeper than Sheol — what can you know?
Its measure is longer than the earth,
and broader than the sea. (Job 11:7-9)

And Eliphaz, another of Job's friends, speaks in the same way as the "Get Wisdom" group who have everything figured out:

You shall come to your grave in ripe old age,
as a shock of grain comes up to the threshing floor in its season.
See, we have searched this out; it is true.
Hear, and know it for yourself. (Job 5:26-27)

But in Job Yahweh says to the friends, "you have not spoken of me what is right" (42:8). The book of Proverbs, then, offers these two positions that are subsequently *discredited*: the first discredited position — God's ways are unknowable, and so one must piously accept all God throws our way; and the second discredited position — that one has it all figured out, and if we just follow these steps all will be well. If those two positions were all one found in the book of Proverbs, it would be a sorry book indeed.

Woman Wisdom

However, I have not yet examined the most compelling and unusual contribution of Proverbs, the portrayal of Woman Wisdom. In Proverbs 1, it says:

Wisdom cries out in the street;
in the squares she raises her voice.
At the busiest corner she cries out;
at the entrance of the city gates she speaks:
"How long, O simple ones, will you love being simple?"
(Prov 1:20-22)

Ḥokmah, the Hebrew word for wisdom, has a feminine ending and here stands personified as a divine figure prophetically calling the simple to her. The author frames her appeal using erotic terms: "Say to wisdom,

'You are my sister,'/and call insight your intimate friend" (7:4).[7] Chapter 8 of Proverbs describes Hokmah's birth: "Yahweh created me at the beginning of his work,/the first of his acts of long ago" (8:22).

The chapter presents Hokmah as an Israelite goddess, the daughter of Yahweh. The poet employs three different terms to describe Hokmah's origin. They are *qanani*, "Yahweh *acquired* me . . ." (8:22); *nissakti*, "I was *poured out*" (8:23); and *holaleti*, "I was *brought forth*" (8:24 and 25). The first, from *qana*, can mean "create," but here it refers to Hokmah's birth, as when Eve named her first son Cain because she had "acquired" from Yahweh a son.[8]

The second word is from *nasak*, "Ages ago I was *poured out*." The NRSV translates *nasak* as "set up," but this term originates from a ceramic process whereby the pot is formed by clay *poured into* a mold. In the case of Hokmah, we might understand the mold as the divine womb, the womb of Yahweh. Compare this to Genesis 2, when Yahweh "formed" the first man as a potter shapes a pot. William F. Albright's alternative interpretation of the word bears repeating. He suggests that *nasak* refers to an "outpouring of generative semen."[9]

The final word, *holaleti*, from the root *hul* or *hil*, refers to the writhing motions of a woman in childbirth. Bernhard Lang makes the observation, "She is not the product of the artisan's skill, nor has she been conquered in battle to be made part of the ordered world. Rather, she has been *born* or

---

7. "Sister" is a pet name for one's sexual companion, as in the Song of Songs: "I come to my garden, my sister, my bride;/I gather my myrrh with my spice,/I eat my honeycomb with my honey,/I drink my wine with my milk./Eat, friends, drink,/and be drunk with love" (Song 5:1).

8. G. M. Landes notes regarding the word *qnny*, "the meaning 'to beget, produce, create,' would seem to be earlier than the much more common 'to buy, acquire, possess'"; "Creation Tradition in Proverbs 8,22-31 and Genesis 1," in *A Light unto My Path*, ed. Howard N. Bream, Ralph D. Heim, and Carey A. Moore (Philadelphia: Temple University Press, 1974), 281. Mitchell Dahood also translates this as "begot"; "Proverbs 8,22-31," *CBQ* 30 (1968): 513. R. N. Whybray concurs: "Although there is only one word that strictly means sexual birth in the passage . . . the other two verbs have alternative meaning that include sexual birth. q-n-h is used in some places to mean 'give birth,' as when Eve says she has 'gotten' a child from the Lord. And 'set up' *nasak* can mean to have been 'woven' together in the womb"; *Proverbs* (NCBC; Grand Rapids: Eerdmans, 1994), 131. See also Helmer Ringgren, *Word and Wisdom* (Lund: Ohlssons, 1947), 101-2.

9. William F. Albright, cited in Bernhard Lang, *Wisdom and the Book of Proverbs: A Hebrew Goddess Redefined* (New York: Pilgrim, 1986), 63.

brought forth by birth. Wisdom says of herself, 'I was born *(holalti),* an expression used to refer to human birth."[10]

"When there were no depths I was *brought forth* . . ." (8:24). The word is used a second time in verse 25: "before the hills, I was *brought forth* . . ." The verses thereby indicate that Yahweh is divine parent, both father and mother. Hokmah existed before all the primal forces arrayed at the beginning of Genesis, "the earth," "the depths," "the heavens," "the mountains." She was there before all of that, playing at Yahweh's feet as a little child.

However, we are not limited to just that cosmic scene. Woman Wisdom pervades much more of Proverbs than these few passages that explicitly mention her. For example, we see her imprint when the sage warns against the "strange woman," the *'ishshah zarah*:

> You will be saved from the loose woman *('ishshah zarah),*
>   from the adulteress with her smooth words,
> who forsakes the partner of her youth
>   and forgets her sacred covenant;
> for her way leads down to death,
>   and her paths to the shades;
> those who go to her never come back,
>   nor do they regain the paths of life. (2:16-19)

Although this passage may be understood (and surely has been understood by some) as a simple exhortation to avoid dangerously seductive women, what prevents us from leaving her there is the mythological language with which the poem concludes. She is not merely a dangerous woman who can destroy a young man's reputation, but rather a demon from hell whose house is a portal to the netherworld.

> Her house is the way to Sheol,
> going down to the chambers of death. (7:27)

Certainly all this can be read as a flat metaphor: "For her way leads down to death" would then mean "You will be really sorry. You will suffer shame and humiliation, loss of status, and the woman's husband will kill

---

10. Lang, *Wisdom,* 63.

you." And the text works as intended on that level. But at the same time the *'ishshah zarah* represents the exact counterpart to Hokmah. In some ways she is her mirror image, her doppelganger, as well as her nemesis. They together struggle over the lives and souls of the young men in their charge, presumably the students and children of wise teachers. Both Hokmah and *'ishshah zarah* seek the same end — to entice the young man to their respective houses, to seduce him. The author prefers Hokmah's house, and gives it glowing praise.

> Wisdom has built her house,
> she has hewn her seven pillars.
> She has slaughtered her animals, she has mixed her wine,
> she has also set her table.
> She has sent out her servant-girls, she calls
> from the highest places in the town,
> "You that are simple, turn in here!"
> To those without sense she says,
> "Come, eat of my bread
> and drink of the wine I have mixed." (9:1-5)

He regards the house of the *'ishshah zarah* as severely dangerous:

> Now in the street, now in the squares,
> and at every corner she lies in wait.
> She seizes him and kisses him,
> and with impudent face she says to him:
> . . .
> I have decked my couch with coverings,
> colored spreads of Egyptian linen;
> I have perfumed my bed with myrrh,
> aloes, and cinnamon.
> Come, let us take our fill of love until morning;
> let us delight ourselves with love. (7:12-18)

But the sage warns:

> for her way leads down to death,
> and her paths to the shades;

those who go to her never come back,
nor do they regain the paths of life. (2:18-19)[11]

The anomaly of a Hebrew goddess in the Bible strikes many. In spite of a movement in Israel towards greater and greater consolidation of divine power in the one god Yahweh, Hokmah retains her presence and influence in Israel, and in Judaism and Christianity that followed. However, the debate rages over what degree of reality one should accord Hokmah. At one extreme some see Hokmah as a dead metaphor, a toothless symbol representing one or another principle. Some suggest that she represents the world, some, divine wisdom. Some, borrowing a term from Christology, speak of her as a hypostasis, an aspect of the divine being, spun off and described as a separate entity. A hypostasis is a way God manifests herself in the world.

At the other extreme are those who understand that the biblical author described a goddess in which he believed and probably worshipped. Alternatively, she could be a literary portrayal of such a goddess. She would be just as real a character in the text, but no one would actually worship her or offer her sacrifice. In either case, the language of Hokmah is goddess language. The author portrays Hokmah as Yahweh's daughter.[12]

What Unity in Proverbs?

I intend to show here how the first two sections, "The Dispute between the 'Fear God' Sages and the 'Get Wisdom' Sages" and my analysis of Woman Wisdom and the *'ishshah zarah,* fit together. Does Hokmah align herself with the "Fear God" sages? The "Get Wisdom" sages? Does she reject both their houses and offer a new understanding? Does she present a skepticism

---

11. See James L. Crenshaw, "Murphy's Axiom: Every Gnomic Saying Needs a Balancing Corrective," in *The Listening Heart: Essays in Wisdom and the Psalms in Honour of Roland E. Murphy, O.Carm,* ed. Kenneth G. Hogland et al. (JSOTSup 58; Sheffield: JSOT, 1987), 13, note 20; and Roland E. Murphy, "Wisdom and Eros in Proverbs 1–9," *CBQ* 50 (1988): 603.

12. Carol R. Fontaine views her as a "repressed archetype," "a literary image of a goddess who had no correspondence in the actual cultic life of sages or anyone else"; "Wisdom in Proverbs," in *In Search of Wisdom: Essays in Memory of John G. Gammie,* ed. Leo G. Perdue, Bernard Brandon Scott, and William Johnston Wiseman (Louisville: Westminster John Knox, 1993), 100; and note 1: ". . . if the figure of Woman Wisdom is viewed as a repressed archetype, she might erupt into consciousness during any period, and would be especially likely to do so in times of social disintegration and reorganization, such as postexilic Israel." See also p. 112.

against all systems? Unfortunately, none of this fits or represents in any way how the authors portray Hokmah in the Bible.

I first attempted to address the unity of Proverbs years ago by treating each collection in Proverbs separately.[13] Proverbs is organized into unequally sized "collections," each with an introduction. But the collections are not significant to the understanding of the book as a whole. Alternatively, one could rearrange the verses of Proverbs according to topics and discuss, for instance, what the book says about childrearing, or how one should speak, or about marriage. But that is not the way the Proverbs were written. Any rubric I employed to understand or organize Proverbs, I have found, was alien to the phenomenon of the book itself.

I always knew one couldn't capture all of Proverbs in a single idea, like "fear God," or "get wisdom," but I thought perhaps I could uncover the "soul" of Proverbs by examining a conflict between these two important ideas. I found, however, that the conflict between the "Get Wisdom" and the "Fear God" groups held little interest or creativity; this conflict necessarily left out huge swaths of the book, and particularly, it leaves no room for Hokmah. And she is an important figure on her own. She is vital for an understanding of Proverbs. She begins and ends the book.[14]

But I cannot develop any overriding rubric. I'm not even sure if I should. But if I don't, then I have two chapters in the place of one.

So if I had two chapters, this is the way I would end them. First, I would end the "Fear God/Get Wisdom" chapter with a discussion of how these two groups are manifestly wrongheaded. They are at best rationalizing, making their precarious theological position more certain by avoiding any challenges. One advises trusting God and giving up on figuring things out. The other has everything figured out and imposes a rigid system to understand the messiness of human life. At worst, they deliberately cover up what they know to be the truth: there is trouble at the heart of their confidence in God. The evil in the world can be neither explained nor tolerated. Instead, they provide half-baked explanations, and that becomes an offense.

Second, in the ending of the Hokmah chapter I would repeat that

---

13. See David Penchansky, "Proverbs," in *Mercer Commentary on the Bible*, ed. Watson E. Mills and Richard F. Wilson (Macon: Mercer University Press, 1995), 193-96.

14. Fontaine notes "that Woman Wisdom is herself the 'root metaphor' that organizes the book as a whole. In fact, as a 'character,' Woman Wisdom receives more treatment than any other female in the Hebrew Bible, and ranks fifth among both male and female characters behind God, Job, Moses, and David"; "Wisdom in Proverbs," 112.

Hokmah is a Hebrew goddess, the daughter of Yahweh. I would consider the implications from such an insight for our understanding of ancient Israelite monotheism.

But how to make the two chapters into one? I fear I cannot. So I present to you, my readers, this conundrum:

Is there anything one can say about this entire book without ignoring an important part? Since the largest unit of meaning in Proverbs is the single verse or couplet, is there anything intelligent that one can say about the entire book? Is it even desirable to have some capsule statement to capture it all? Isn't that what the "Get Wisdom" and "Fear Yahweh" groups tried to do? They tried to capture all the wisdom enterprise in a single concept. It didn't work for them either.

Therefore, I surrender to the formlessness of the book that has successfully resisted my efforts to impose any kind of shape. There is a reason why, in writing this introduction, I left the book of Proverbs for last. Ultimately, it has defeated me, and I say with Agur:

> I am weary, O God,
> . . . How can I prevail?
> Surely I am too stupid to be human;
> I do not have human understanding.
> I have not learned wisdom,
> nor have I knowledge of the holy ones. (30:1-3)

QUESTIONS FOR REVIEW

Q Is the book of Proverbs a unified work?

Q Who are the different groups responsible for the book of Proverbs?

Q How was Woman Wisdom born?

Q Is Hokmah a Hebrew goddess?

Q Does Penchansky succeed in describing a unifying principle for the whole of Proverbs? Why or why not? Do you agree?

KEY WORDS

- "Fear God"
- "Get Wisdom"
- *Hokmah*
- Woman Wisdom
- Foreign woman
- Agur

FOR FURTHER READING

Fontaine, Carole R. "Wisdom in Proverbs." In *In Search of Wisdom: Essays in Memory of John G. Gammie,* ed. Leo G. Perdue, Bernard Brandon Scott, and William Johnston Wiseman. Louisville: Westminster John Knox, 1993, 99-114.

Penchansky, David. "Proverbs." In *Mercer Commentary on the Bible,* ed. Watson E. Mills and Richard F. Wilson. Macon: Mercer University Press, 1995, 193-96.

3. The Meaning of the Book of Job

He still persists in his integrity, although you incited me against him,
to destroy him for no reason.

JOB 2:3

. . . for you have not spoken of me what is right, as my servant Job
has.

JOB 42:7

The problem of undeserved evil is so much a part of human experience that there is never a time in history where people did not struggle over this. Many regarded the world governed by capricious gods who had to be appeased, but whose favor was never assured. In contrast to this, some, early in Israel's history, suggested new and radical ideas about deity. This particular god, their national god, was fair, faithful, and just. They went further and suggested that Yahweh was in fact benevolent and merciful. Nevertheless, undeserved evil continued always as the theological knot they found too difficult to untie. The book of Job remains one of the most profound and complex attempts by the Israelites, through their sages, to address the problem.

The Structure of Job: Overview

Job divides into three uneven sections. The Prologue (chs. 1 and 2) and the Epilogue (42:7-17) are written mostly in a once-upon-a-time kind of prose, narrative in form. If one splits the present book of Job open, removes the center and puts the Prologue and Epilogue together, the story reads smoothly and makes sense. Many suggest, and I agree, that these three chapters constitute an older form of the book and that a later editor, or more likely editors, divided the work and inserted a lengthy commentary in the center.[1] The Prologue depicts Job's original state of blessedness, wealth, renown, with a complete family. The scene shifts from heaven, where Yahweh and the Satan gamble over Job's fate, to the earth, where Job suffers yet remains faithful. He "did not sin with his lips."

The center consists of two different parts. The bulk of it constitutes a debate between Job and his friends. His friends, in the Prologue, have come to comfort Job in his sufferings. Job cries out in anger against God who has afflicted him, and the friends rush to God's defense. The author roughly structures the debates in three cycles. Job takes the floor once in response to each of the friends' speeches.[2]

Many have tried to discern a progression in the arguments between Job and his friends, but I see none. There are distinctions and subtleties between the friends' various monologues, but they all roughly make the same point: that God would not afflict Job in such a manner if he were innocent. We cannot, save by the most strenuous readings, (a) make a distinction between the positions of the different friends; or (b) determine a progression in the debate, either in tone (from less to more angry/strident) or in ideas. The friends are interchangeable in their arguments, and Job's position changes only once in the debate — he turns from the friends in frustration and increasingly focuses his questions and protests of innocence towards God.

In the second part of the book's center, "the speeches of Yahweh,"

1. Probably leaving some parts out from the original Ur-story.
2. Every cycle should have six parts, three for Job and each of the friends one. However, the third cycle does not follow this pattern. The last speech of the friend Bildad is missing, and some of Job's speeches are short and not characteristic of his positions. Perhaps some damage occurred to the text, a copyist error, or maybe we see evidence of some deep design of the narrator. Some have suggested (without good foundation, in my opinion) that the degradation of the last cycle is a way for the author to indicate that the argument itself has degraded.

Yahweh appears and speaks to Job out of a whirlwind. There are two cycles of speeches. Each begins when Yahweh challenges Job, and each ends when Job utterly capitulates under Yahweh's forceful arguments and thunderous anger. The book ends with an Epilogue where Yahweh restores Job's health, his wealth, standing in the community, and gives him new children. The fairy-tale conclusion parallels the book's beginning, the ancient Israelite equivalent of "happily ever after":

> After this Job lived for one hundred and forty years, and saw his children, and his children's children, four generations. And Job died, old and full of days. (Job 42:16-17)

The Prologue

The Prologue of the book of Job portrays Yahweh ruling over a council consisting of divine beings. The silent chorus known as the *bene 'elohim* appear in heaven, presenting themselves to Yahweh.[3] Another figure appears *with* the *bene 'elohim,* known in Hebrew as *ha-satan.* The addition of the definite article in Hebrew, *the* Satan, indicates this is not a name but a title. The verbal root *sin-tet-nun* indicates "one who opposes," so the term frequently has been translated "the adversary."

Ha-satan appears *with* the *bene 'elohim,* which gives a sense that he is one of them, and yet the text treats him apart and separate. Yahweh singles him out as well, directing his speech towards the Satan alone, ignoring the others. The Satan had traveled the earth on a quest which the narrator never fully explains. He has been ". . . going to and fro on the earth, and . . . walking up and down on it" (1:7). It appears his role was like Diogenes, who searched for a single person whose honesty was beyond question. It appears that the Satan searched for one whose devotion to Yahweh was utter and complete.[4] He was to examine the piety of all

---

3. This phrase might be translated: "the sons/children of God"; "the sons/children of the *'elohim*"; "the class of being known as *'elohim,* divine beings." For a discussion, see my *Twilight of the Gods: Polytheism in the Hebrew Bible* (Louisville: Westminster John Knox, 2005), chs. 5 and 6.

4. This is implied by the fact that the Satan roams the earth (no one explains the purpose of these wanderings), that Yahweh pointed out the piety of Job, and by the Satan's subsequent calling into question of Job's righteousness.

Yahweh's subjects and then report back to the head of the divine council, Yahweh.

But there exists an undercurrent of personal competition between these two, Yahweh and the Satan. We join them in the middle of a long-standing dispute. It would appear that in previous meetings Yahweh had pointed out various humans he regarded as righteous, and in each case the Satan had been able to demonstrate how they fell short. Yahweh and *ha-satan* argue as equals, save for the fact that the lesser deity must receive permission and is given limits at every stage of his activities.[5]

And now, finally, Yahweh has found someone with whom the Satan will not be able to find fault. Yahweh has eagerly awaited the Satan's appearance so he would be able to point out this one who will certainly withstand the accuser's scrutiny. This one, Job, Yahweh tells him, is "blameless and upright . . . fears God and turns away from evil" (1:8).[6] Thus he repeats the words the narrator had used to introduce Job (1:1).

The Satan can find no fault with Job's behavior. He therefore changes the standards by which Job would be judged. It is no longer enough that Job observes all his religious obligations with annoying scrupulosity, nor that he generously protects the poor and marginalized in his society. Now Yahweh must also demonstrate that he does all these with no expectation of reward. The Satan utters a challenge:

> "Does Job fear God for nothing? . . . You have blessed the work of his hands, and his possessions have increased in the land. But stretch out your hand now, and touch all that he has, and he will curse you to your face." (1:9-11)

Job is singularly blessed with children, property, and reputation, which everyone including Job believes is the result of his exemplary behavior. By taking away Job's blessings, Yahweh and the Satan will determine whether or not Job's behavior depends upon an immediate reward. Yahweh takes the challenge, and this transaction between the two of them can best be understood as a wager. If Job, bereft of his blessings, curses God, that will prove that he only acts holy for the rewards that he gets. If

---

5. *Ha-satan* scarcely resembles the figure of Satan from later Jewish and Christian sources.

6. These four terms (perfect, upright, fears God, and turns away from evil) mean roughly the same thing.

he refuses to curse but instead worships Yahweh, Yahweh then would win the bet.[7]

After losing his children and his wealth, Job says, "the LORD gave and the LORD has taken away; blessed be the name of the LORD" (1:21). Yahweh indeed has won the bet. Even though Yahweh has taken away everything Job has, the man continues to worship. This worship does not depend upon an expectation of reward.

The Satan returns to heaven at a designated time, along with the *bene 'elohim,* and Yahweh again boasts about Job.[8] He says:

"[Job] still persists in his integrity, although you incited me against him, to destroy him for no reason." (2:3)

What an astounding statement! Yahweh admits that the Satan "incited" him to afflict Job "with no cause." "Incited" (Heb. *sut*) means to persuade someone to sin. The ancient rabbis said, "Were it not written in the Bible it would be impossible to say: God is like a man whom someone tries to incite and who is in the end incited."[9]

The term translated "for no reason" (Heb. *ḥinnam*) should be considered as well. There was (according to Yahweh) no value or benefit in what Yahweh had done in allowing the Satan to murder Job's children and destroy his wealth. The Satan had tricked Yahweh into sinning when he consented to afflict Job in a useless, gratuitous act of cruelty. After Yahweh realized what an evil thing he had done, allowing Job to suffer just so he could win a bet, *the Satan convinces him to do it again,* only worse. With Yahweh's permission, the Satan covers Job with loathsome sores over his whole body and leaves him scratching himself on an ash dump. Yahweh in the story is gullible and impulsive, capable of thoughtless cruelty in order to win in an intellectual argument with his friend.

---

7. Those who argue that it is not a bet seem to do so because the notion of Yahweh placing a bet offends their sensibilities. The alternate explanation is that what we have is a self-curse, that the Satan calls a curse upon himself (consequences unnamed) if Job cannot be made to curse God. But that is still a bet. The curse is the payment the Satan will face if he loses the bet.

8. Perhaps the curse, the penalty for the Satan if he lost the bet, was to listen to Yahweh gloat over the victory.

9. Quoted in Meir Weiss, *The Story of Job's Beginning: Job 1-2, A Literary Analysis* (Jerusalem: Magnes, 1983), 37.

The Center Section of Job: The Debate and Yahweh's Speeches

Matitiahu Tsevat points out that the wager is only a set-up for the more significant controversies addressed by the book later on. I copied the title of this chapter, "The Meaning of the Book of Job," as an allusion and homage to his influential essay published in 1966.[10] Tsevat had the audacity to try and gather the diverse voices in this complex book of Job, produced over centuries of intense textual activity, and organize them into a single theme or message.

The Satan afflicts Job, and then Job argues with his friends. Finally, he turns away from his friends and challenges God to justify his affliction of Job, and God appears to him in a whirlwind.[11] Tsevat says that all this enables the author to address the issue of undeserved suffering.

Job's suffering is completely undeserved. Three times we are told that Job is blameless, upright, fears God, and turns away from evil (once from the narrator, twice from Yahweh). Job's sufferings are caused by Yahweh's desire to best the Satan and had nothing to do with any real or imagined deficiencies in Job's piety. He had absolutely no idea regarding any of the events that took place in heaven. These disasters came upon him suddenly with no warning, and he tries to make sense of this destructive turn his life has taken. Because of these experiences, Job claims his suffering is undeserved. As Tsevat insists, both Job and his friends expect God to reward good behavior and punish the bad. So Job's affliction must be explained somehow.

The friends do not believe that suffering could be undeserved. For them, suffering always had to have an explanation. Through human suffering God enforces the strictures of his moral universe. According to the friends, God is forever and always punishing people with great and tiny

10. Matitiahu Tsevat, "The Meaning of the Book of Job," *HUCA* 37 (1966): 73-106.

11. David Clines divides the many interpretations of Job into three main categories (a fourth is not useful): "1) the ideal patient man, piously and fatalistically accepting his suffering as the will of God. . . .; 2) the champion of reason against dogma, of empirical observation against tradition. . . .; 3) the victim of a cruel and absurd world . . . that finds even in the divine speeches a defense of a cosmic irrationality"; David J. A. Clines, "Why Is There a Book of Job and What Does It Do to You If You Read It?" in *The Book of Job,* ed. W. A. M. Beuken (Leuven: Leuven University Press, 1994), 15. Tsevat would not put it that way, but he argues that the speeches of Yahweh are a defense of divine irrationality, as I will explain below. That is the third of Clines's interpretations.

misfortunes as a consequence for their infractions against the moral and ritual law.

That humans suffer there is no doubt. But if all their suffering is deserved, then there is no theological problem to be solved. The universe would remain balanced and orderly. With that in mind, the friends articulate the reasons why Job deserves his suffering. They suggest different things: hubris, some secret sin, the fact that Job shares the imperfection of all created beings, for even the angels have imperfections. Finally they accuse him of speaking disrespectfully concerning Yahweh. All these accusations come from the same place — it is inconceivable that Yahweh would allow undeserved suffering. That would mean either that Yahweh was not all powerful or that he was not all good. So the suffering must be something the sufferer brought on her or himself.

In the course of debating with his friends, Job accuses Yahweh of cruelty. Consider the following examples from Job's speeches in the book's center:

"The arrows of the Almighty are in me . . .
the terrors of God are arrayed against me." (6:4)

"Will you not . . . let me be until I swallow my spittle?
Why have you made me a target?" (7:19-20)

"For he crushes me with a tempest,
and multiplies my wounds without cause." (9:17)

"Bold as a lion you hunt me." (10:16)

"Who among all these does not know
that the hand of Yahweh has done this?" (12:9)

"He has torn me in his wrath, and hated me;
he has gnashed his teeth at me." (16:9) [a threatening, aggressive gesture]

Job finds himself increasingly frustrated with the friends and their efforts to defend Yahweh, and more and more he turns towards Yahweh as the only one who can either vindicate Job or declare to all what Job has done to deserve such treatment. In his last speech, Job turns towards Yahweh and declares his innocence in sacred oath. Job begins by speaking of a legal trial that would determine his guilt or innocence. He attacks Yahweh at the very point where the reader (and presumably Yahweh himself) knows that Yahweh is in fact guilty. Yahweh did indeed afflict Job, even though Job was innocent of any wrongdoing. So even though the trial Job wants is a trial which determines his (that is, Job's) innocence, by implication, Job also wants to put Yahweh on trial for treating his servant so unfairly.

Yahweh is already guilty, only Job and the friends had not witnessed the incriminating wager. Because of Yahweh's guilt, he reacts defensively and in anger:

> "Shall a faultfinder contend with the Almighty?
> Anyone who argues with God must respond." (40:2)

> "Will you even put me in the wrong?
> Will you condemn me that you may be justified?" (40:8)

Tsevat reads the entire book of Job from the perspective of these speeches of Yahweh. He claims that they provide a key to its understanding. In agreement with him, most interpreters assert that Yahweh's speeches provide the climax and the answer to Job's questions. There are strong reasons for making this claim. Yahweh's appearance to explain things is what Job has been longing for in his more forceful moments. It is what he demands in his final speech, which he directs towards heaven.

> "Oh, that I had one to hear me!
> (Here is my signature! let the Almighty answer me!)
> Oh, that I had the indictment written by my adversary!
> Surely I would carry it on my shoulder;
> I would bind it on me like a crown;
> I would give him an account of all my steps;
> like a prince I would approach him." (31:35-37)

Further, Yahweh's voice has established authority — so what he says to Job would constitute a reliable answer to his questions. Additionally, the way Job ultimately responds to Yahweh's speeches (see below) suggests that they have completely transformed his attitudes and ideas.

Even those interpreters who defend Job against attacks of wrongdoing, who consider Job an innocent sufferer, rush to agree that Job needed a corrective lesson in humility and that it did him some good. They all agree that Job was fundamentally wrong in his understanding of the way God and the universe worked. Job must learn that his petty concern for justice and fairness has little to do with how God governs the universe.

Yahweh in his speeches points to the wild animals he sustains. "Who provides for the raven its prey,/when its young ones cry to God,/and wander about for lack of food?" (38:41) For Tsevat, this means that Yahweh's scope of attention is wider and different from a human's perspective. Contrariwise, I see the wild animals as another way Yahweh boasts that he can do what is far beyond Job's capabilities. This is another way that Yahweh claims superiority and thus declares that only an equal has the right to bring accusations against the divine. That is the content and theme of Yahweh's speeches, contrary to Tsevat, and contrary to Job's hopeful expectations for a *go'el* to defend him. (19:25)

Reading the book of Job through the lens of the speeches of Yahweh, Tsevat determines that the figure of Job had somehow wronged Yahweh and that his ideas about God needed correction. Job had to learn on some deep existential level (because he knew it all already on the level of belief) that Yahweh is stronger than he, that Yahweh has been around much longer than he had, and that Yahweh has more important things to do than to worry about Job's minor complaints. Job learned that Yahweh could crush him like a bug any time he wanted.

In response to Yahweh's appearance, Job finally says, "I had heard of you by the hearing of the ear,/but now my eye sees you" (42:5). Tsevat says that "the hearing of the ear" is a reference to Israel's accumulated wisdom, the tradition passed down from previous generations of sages. Hearing alone proves inadequate, according to Job.

How foolish and self-centered of Job to think that his outrage at undeserved suffering would have any meaning from God's perspective. It matters not that Job feels innocent — he has truly stepped over the line by accusing Yahweh of unrighteousness. Gods and goddesses do not bend to the whims and concerns of mortals. Humans must always show the proper respect to the gods, and this Job has failed to do in his accusations against Yahweh. Yahweh claims that Job must not base his piety on desire for reward or fear of punishment. Rather, it is gratuitous, out of love and devotion to a God that does little or nothing on his behalf.

Tsevat paraphrases and summarizes Yahweh's rebuke of Job:

"Are you so wrapped up in yourself as to be closed to all else? Or would you now perhaps admit the possible existence and validity of standards of which you had not dreamed . . . ?"[12]

For Tsevat, Yahweh's speeches answer Job's questions, so although it might seem to Job that God had been cruel to him, in reality this was only God's inattention because Job is not that important in the grand scheme of things. God cannot be limited by notions of reward and punishment, human good and evil. Tsevat continues:

God is not only infinitely mightier but also wiser than [Job]. God's is that inscrutable business, the government of the world. While man thinks only of his own needs and problems, God sustains a whole world, providing for all his creatures.[13]

He goes on to say:

In the natural world, where the category of cause and effect is operative, man is not as central as you fancy. . . . Divine justice is not an element of reality. It is a figment existing only in the misguided philosophy with which you have been inculcated.[14]

Do the Speeches Satisfy Job?

Is Job transformed by Yahweh's speeches? Does Job see the error of his ways? On the contrary, Job does not receive satisfaction. Rather, God bullied him to withdraw his accusation. Tsevat thinks that Yahweh's speeches have instructive value in spite of the fact that they neither address Job's questions nor does Yahweh inform Job regarding the true reason for Job's suffering, the wager between Yahweh and the Satan. Rather than being transformed by the speeches, Job is first silenced and then forced to say whatever it is that God insists upon hearing.

I question the sincerity of Job's capitulation. Yahweh speaks for two whole chapters, challenging Job's qualifications to bring charges against de-

12. Tsevat, "The Meaning of the Book of Job," 89.
13. Tsevat, "The Meaning of the Book of Job," 93.
14. Tsevat, "The Meaning of the Book of Job," 100.

ity. Consequently, Job collapses in fear: "I lay my hand on my mouth. I have spoken once and I will not answer" (40:4-5). Yahweh accuses and challenges Job for two additional chapters, eliciting a second recantation, more wrenching and self-abasing than the first: "I *despise* myself," he says. "I repent in dust and ashes" (42:6). Of what value is such a confession, after facing four chapters of divine rebuke? Job's recantation was bullied and coerced.[15]

Tsevat and many others claim that the divine speeches remove Job from the center of his own existence. This is a near universal insight, and one that I cannot accept. Why is it a good thing for Job's pain to be rendered unimportant? Job's suffering is profound, striking deep at every level of his being, and we (the readers) know that his suffering is ill-placed and unfair because undeserved. Is it better for the sufferer to be silenced because he learns he is not the center of the universe? Is that how one should speak to a person who experiences crushing disease, betrayal, and loss? Rather, it is insensitive and insulting to Job and the dignity of his suffering to remind him that God regards his pain as insignificant in the grand scheme of things. Edwin Good well characterizes the speeches of Yahweh:

> Yet the divine speeches are full of a lordly rhetorical sarcasm that brutally puts Job down, and interpreters seem eager to assist in that process. Are we afraid of the daring example of the person who stands up and argues human importance and dignity? Do we, like the friends, feel that Job's suffering indicates that he deserved what he got and that his feistiness against the god compounds a felony whose basis we never know?[16]

Therefore, I suggest an alternative to reading the book, not through the lens of the speeches. Rather, when one reads the book of Job through the lens of 42:7, the book takes on a different character. At the outset of the Epilogue, Yahweh addresses Eliphaz as representative of the three friends

15. James L. Crenshaw is troubled by the implications of Job's repentance: "An innocent Job smarts from God's challenge, 'Will you even put me in the wrong? Will you condemn me that you may be justified?' (Job 40:8), and [Job] proceeds to reverse the offense by putting himself in the wrong. Standing before this blustering deity, such a one can only repent in dust and ashes. Where then is his integrity? Has not peace been purchased at too great a cost?"; "The Shift from Theodicy to Anthropodicy," in *Theodicy in the Old Testament* (IRT 4; Philadelphia: Fortress and London: SPCK, 1983), 9.

16. Edwin M. Good, *In Turns of Tempest: A Reading of Job* (Stanford: Stanford University Press, 1990), 368.

45

and says to him: ". . . you have not spoken of me what is right,[17] as my servant Job has." Yahweh holds that these true words of Job contrast with what the friends had said. Their words were not true. Job's declarations of innocence are true, and 42:7 validates his accusations against Yahweh. That means Yahweh's speeches were not right, because *they* say exactly the opposite of Job's truth, that Job had no right to declare his innocence nor to accuse God, not being Yahweh's equal. Reading the entire book through the lens of 42:7 invalidates Job's two earlier recantations. Why should Job take back statements he made in the center, if they are true according to Yahweh's final statement?[18]

In the debates, Job declares that he is innocent of any wrong that would merit the degree of suffering that he experiences. Job accuses God of poorly governing the world, allowing great injustice to continue.[19] The friends insist that Job must be guilty of something and that God must (by definition, as a ground rule) be innocent of all wrongdoing. So we are then left in the difficult position where God declares as true Job's characterization that God unjustly pursues and destroys him. Further, we must then struggle with the fact that Yahweh in his speeches (chs. 38–41) declares Job an arrogant usurper of divine power. He insists that Job has no right to accuse God of anything unless he can attain equality with God's power and ability. Now, according to Yahweh's characterization in the book's Epilogue (42:7), what Yahweh said in the speeches must be all wrong.

Job 42:7 is the last summative comment in the book regarding Job's questions and his predicament. The verses that follow are narrative and obscure in their meaning. Job is restored and ends his life in blessedness. So 42:7 is the last explicit comment on the meaning of the story. By this I mean that one can read 42:7 as God's final word and final act.

---

17. Heb. *nekonah* means "true" or "right."

18. Crenshaw questions the true nature of Job's repentance: "In a real sense, Job's silent submission before an awesome display of power amounts to loss of integrity, hence may rightly be termed an argument against humanity. It may actually be the case that self-abnegation lies at the heart of all theodicy. Only as the individual fades into nothingness can the deity achieve absolute pardon"; "The Shift from Theodicy to Anthropodicy," 6.

19. In Psalm 82, Yahweh accuses the other gods of improperly governing the world — these deities were therefore demoted, cast down from heaven, and condemned to mortality. Now Job accuses Yahweh of the same offense. See my *Twilight of the Gods: Polytheism in the Hebrew Bible* (Louisville: Westminster John Knox, 2005), ch. 6, for an analysis of Yahweh's judgment upon the other gods.

Some suggest that the words of Job to which Yahweh refers speak not of his arguments in the center, but rather his pious statements of trust in the Prologue[20] or his forced recantation at the end. In other words, Job spoke the truth when he said, "Yahweh takes away. Blessed be Yahweh's name" (1:21), or when he said, "I despise myself" (42:6). However, I strongly argue that they refer to Job's statements in debate with his friends, because that is the contrast that Yahweh himself makes. What the friends say is not right, Yahweh says, while Job's words speak truth about God.

Yahweh's endorsement of Job's side in the argument throws the entire interpretation of the book of Job into a tailspin. Job's speech accuses God of failing in his governance of the universe, because he persecuted Job like a ravening monster. Yahweh endorses this particular message as the *truth* about him. The friends argued that it was impossible for God to ever be in the wrong. They defended God's integrity and justice. Yahweh declares those statements to be not true.

There remains this further indication that Job's accusations stand un-answered at the book's close. Yahweh's restoration of Job without a word of apology or regret is offensive and insensitive. God's acts of restoration are the actions of one who feels bad but does not want to say, "I'm sorry." Job remains silent during his restoration. Might that silence be a mute protest against one whose supreme power has abused and used Job disgracefully in order to win a bet, to take a dare or a challenge?[21] I hope so.

Experience and Tradition: The Conflict in the Wisdom Movement

The Israelite wisdom tradition passed down by the sages taught that God governed the universe with justice and fairness and enforced the principles of wisdom through inevitable consequences for significant moral decisions. Human experience, however, argues that many times people who do evil escape the consequences for their actions and many people who suffer have done nothing wrong to deserve that suffering. Job's experience leads him to

20. "Yahweh gave. Yahweh has taken away. Blessed be Yahweh's name" (1:21); "Shall we receive the good at the hand of God, and not receive the bad?" (2:10).

21. For another example of silent protest against unjust deity, note how Aaron says nothing to Moses after his sons are killed by Yahweh in Leviticus 10. See my discussion in *What Rough Beast: Images of God in the Hebrew Bible* (Louisville: Westminster John Knox, 1999), ch. 4.

reject the principle of retribution, which is part of the sapiential tradition handed down. Job (the person, not the book) insists that his experience must be taken into account in the interpretation of things that happen. As Mrs. Loman says in *Death of a Salesman,* "Attention must be paid."

The cruel joke of the book is that Job's suffering has nothing to do with punishment for his sin. Job demands that the friends tell him what he did to deserve this. He then demands the same of God. But there is no possible answer to this question. Nothing he did merited this treatment. It was the result of a bet, a cruel experiment. And the bet, the "true" cause of Job's suffering, never comes up again, either in the discussions between the friends, in Yahweh's response to Job's challenge, or in the Epilogue. For Yahweh to have admitted the bet and the gratuitous nature of Job's suffering (as Yahweh admitted to the Satan — "although you incited me against him, to destroy him for no good reason," 2:3) would have made deity look stupid.

Conclusion

So what have we learned? First, there are many voices in Job. The reader must decide which portion and which voice to listen to, in order to produce a meaning from the book. One part of Job, one perspective, when chosen, will be the means by which one interprets the whole. Depending on which portion and voice one chooses, Job will yield an entirely new meaning. How does one choose which voice to use as an analytical fulcrum?

Tsevat chooses to locate the meaning of Job in Yahweh's speeches (chs. 38–41), where Yahweh rebukes Job for his hubris — therefore, Tsevat offers an interpretive narrative in which Job transforms from a person ignorant and presumptuous to one humbled and newly aware of his place in the universe in relation to Yahweh. This narrative requires that Job's final response be abject self-humiliation and deep repentance — "I despise myself, and repent in dust and ashes."

I suggest rather reading the passage through Yahweh's statement in 42:7, where Yahweh says to the friends, "You have not spoken of me what is right, as my servant Job has." Yahweh here refers to the words of Job in the center, where he attacks Yahweh's unfair persecution of his faithful servant. Through this lens, the opening Prologue reads as an unfair attack on an innocent family so that Yahweh might win a bet. The friends' argument, in which they defend the integrity of Yahweh, is profoundly wrongheaded, and Job's most extreme protests continue to stand as accusations against any who might claim the goodness and generosity of God.

Finally, Job's restoration constitutes the final slap in Job's face and Job's silence his mute and ineffective protest against Yahweh's presumption.

QUESTIONS FOR REVIEW

Q Is there a progression in the arguments of the friends?

Q Does the book of Job end happily?

Q Is Satan in the book of Job the same as Satan in the New Testament? How do you know?

Q Is Job's suffering undeserved? How do you know?

Q Does Job curse God?

Q Was Job's capitulation to God sincere?

Q What is the significance of Yahweh's speeches?

Q What is the significance of Job 42:7?

KEY WORDS

– Prologue, Epilogue, Poetic Center

– *bene 'elohim*

– *ha-satan*

FOR FURTHER READING

Crenshaw, James L. *A Whirlpool of Torment: Israelite Traditions of God as an Oppressive Presence.* OBT 12. Philadelphia: Fortress, 1984.
Penchansky, David. *The Betrayal of God: Ideological Conflict in Job.* Louisville: Westminster John Knox, 1990.
Tsevat, Matitiahu. "The Meaning of the Book of Job." *HUCA* 37 (1966): 73-106.

4. Wisdom, Madness, and Folly: The Three Qoheleths

Vanity of vanities, says the Teacher,
vanity of vanities! All is vanity.
What do people gain from all the toil
at which they toil under the sun?

ECCLESIASTES 1:2-3

The end of the matter; all has been heard. Fear God, and keep his
commandments; for that is the whole duty of everyone. For God will
bring every deed into judgment, including every secret thing,
whether good or evil.

ECCLESIASTES 12:13-14

E veryone tries to make sense of the book of Ecclesiastes. Its interpretive difficulties derive from its three distinct voices. Each voice has its own perspective and its own unique theology.[1] Most interpreters want to make one of those voices the "authentic" voice of Qoheleth. I am no exception. But before I do that, I will first examine each of the voices, and briefly survey the various strategies by which readers integrate and reconcile the differences between the three. Finally, I will suggest my own strategy for reading the book. Whether or not these separate voices come from a single

1. Each of these three "Qoheleths" is both a character in the book and its implied author.

author, multiple authors, or pious editors, they represent a sophisticated literary effort to communicate complex and subtle ideas through the presentation of opposites.

These are the three voices within Ecclesiastes: First is *Pessimistic Qoheleth,* who declares, "All is vanity, absurdity." There is no profit or value in living, he says. Pessimistic Qoheleth has his own theology. "God is in heaven," he advises his readers, "and you upon earth; therefore let your words be few" (5:2). Pessimistic Qoheleth's God is capricious. He says, ". . . the righteous and the wise and their deeds are in the hand of God; whether it is love or hate one does not know" (9:1).

The second voice is *Fear God Qoheleth,* similar to the pious voice in the book of Proverbs — God lays down commands, punishes evildoers, and expects people to fear him. Finally, the third voice, is *Enjoy Life Qoheleth,* for whom divinity is accepting and life-affirming, giving humans pleasure and enjoyment. For this Qoheleth, God commands the people to find joy in basic pleasures. Enjoy Life Qoheleth assures his readers, "God has long ago approved what you do" (9:7).

The Voices

The First Voice: Pessimistic Qoheleth

"'Vanity of vanities,' says Pessimistic Qoheleth. 'All is vanity.'" This repeated phrase functions as a kind of motto or thesis statement to summarize how Pessimistic Qoheleth wants the book to be read. Throughout the book, this same Hebrew word, *hebel,* occurs as a kind of refrain. Here I use the traditional translation "vanity."[2]

The word comes from the sound a breath makes, *hebel.*[3] Then, by ex-

2. As KJV, RSV, NRSV. Except where indicated, I will use the NRSV translation. I will transliterate "Qoheleth" rather than use these versions' choice, "The Teacher." Timothy Polk observes, "Indeed, there is scarcely a topic in the book to which *hebel* is not applied . . . the effect of this ubiquitous label is to cast a gloomy pall over all the subjects to which it is applied . . . the entire book seems to stand under its aura of negativity"; "The Wisdom of Irony: A Study of *Hebel* and Its Relation to Joy and Fear of God in Ecclesiastes," *SBTh* 6 (1976): 6-7. See also Douglas B. Miller, "Qohelet's Symbolic Use of HBL," *JBL* 117 (1998): 443.

3. Kiel Seybold, הֶבֶל ,הָבַל, *TDOT* 3 (1978): 314; William H. U. Anderson, *Qoheleth and Its Pessimistic Theology: Hermeneutical Struggles in Wisdom Literature* (Mellen Biblical Press Series 54; Lewiston: Mellen Biblical, 1997), 13.

tension, it means "breath" or "vapor," having the sense of something insubstantial, and occasionally something "not real."[4] But in Ecclesiastes, we cannot nail down a definitive meaning or translation for *hebel*. Or rather, we might say that it means different things in different places. There is no corresponding English word that comes even close to covering all its uses. Michael Fox argues persuasively for translating *hebel* as "absurdity," but even that leaves out the negative moral sense.[5] *Hebel*, you see, is twice mentioned with a phrase employing the word r^c (meaning "evil" or "disaster") — in the first instance (4:8) translating *hebel 'inyan* as "an unhappy business" (NSRV) or "a terrible preoccupation"[6] and in the second instance (6:2) "a grievous ill" (NRSV) or "a terrible sickness."[7] Because of the negative context of so many uses of the term, Fox's translation ("absurdity") is not adequate.

Pessimistic Qoheleth uses *hebel* as his repeating chorus. Following the introduction, it occurs first in 1:14: "I saw all the deeds that are done under the sun; and see, all is vanity and a chasing after wind."

> I said to myself . . . "enjoy yourself." . . . But again, this also was vanity. (2:1)
> So I hated life . . . for all is vanity and a chasing after wind. (2:17)
> This also is vanity and an unhappy business. (4:8)
> This is vanity; it is a grievous ill. (6:2)

Featured also in chapters 7, 8, 11, and 12, *hebel* occurs thirty-eight times in total.[8]

All the uses of *hebel* are negative. Qoheleth calls some things or activities *hebel* because they end with death, or because of some unresolved injustice, or because it did not satisfy, or because life's meanings are impossible for humans to figure out. *Hebel* parallels "chasing after wind,"[9] a pointless, ineffectual activity.

---

4. Isaiah used the same word when he called the idols that the people worship *hebel* (Isa 57:13).

5. Michael V. Fox, "The Meaning of *Hebel* for Qohelet," *JBL* 105 (1986): 409.

6. Choon-Leong Seow, *Ecclesiastes* (AB 18C; New York: Doubleday, 1997), 181.

7. Seow, *Ecclesiastes*, 202.

8. E.g., 6:9; 7:6; 8:10, 14; 11:8, 10; 12:8.

9. Or "feeding on the wind" or "shepherding the wind." The ultimate meaning remains a pointless, ineffectual activity.

Hebel habalim, "vanity of vanities," is a form of the Hebrew superlative, the strongest expression of *hebel.* That Qoheleth expresses this superlative three times in a single sentence (*hebel habalim,* "vanity of vanities" twice and *kol hebel,* "*all* is vanity" once) emphasizes its significance as an interpretive key to the whole of the book. This statement begins Qoheleth's message (1:2), and the same message is repeated at the close of Qoheleth's discourse: "Vanity of vanities, says Qoheleth; all is vanity" (12:8).

Qoheleth declares all things to be *hebel* and then examines wisdom, pleasure, companionship, fame, and wealth to see if they will support this claim. In each case, the desired object (wisdom, pleasure, etc.) turns out indeed to be *hebel.* Qoheleth notes that they lose value when one dies. There is no fairness or logic in how things turn out. These *hebel* comments are spaced uniformly throughout the book, addressing a wide variety of situations. They thus support the assertion which frames the whole, that "all is *hebel.*"[10]

This first voice, Pessimistic Qoheleth, opposed the tenets of traditional wisdom theology and other deeply held religious beliefs of his people: He rejected the notion that God will punish the wicked and reward the righteous. He rejected the notion that humans were above (better than, having authority over) the animals. He rejected the notion that God was a just judge. In 7:15 he writes, "There are righteous people who perish in their righteousness, and there are wicked people who prolong their life in their evildoing."[11] Every single thing that humans can devise leads to hard, unrewarding, unprofitable, difficult labor, and no one will ever understand why they must labor for so little reward. Those who enjoy bounty might lose it at any moment. Everyone loses life's good things at death.

Pessimistic Qoheleth was a sage, disillusioned with the traditions he had been taught. Wisdom has always derived its information through a subtle combination of careful observation and passed-down traditions. For Qoheleth, his own observations of nature and human lives have caused him to question the tradition which taught that God governed the

10. "Qohelet is adamant and insisting with respect to his conclusion that all is absurd and there is no textual reason to doubt the scope of his indictment: rather it refers to every single thing in life"; Benjamin Lyle Berger, "Qohelet and the Exigencies of the Absurd," *BibInt* 9 (2001): 159, note 42.

11. "There are wicked people who are treated according to the conduct of the righteous" (8:14). "The same fate comes to all, to the righteous and the wicked, to the good and the evil. . . . As are the good, so are the sinners" (9:2).

universe in an orderly manner. The sages believed that a "wise" person might discern that order and, by acting according to that knowledge, secure a good and prosperous life. On many levels, and for many reasons, "Pessimistic" Qoheleth vehemently denied this assertion. He was not the first one to question these verities, but he did it in a most sustained and pointed way.

The Second Voice: Fear God Qoheleth

The book's conclusion, its epilogue, shifts to the third person and describes Qoheleth and summarizes his teaching: "The end of the matter; [it says] all has been heard. Fear God, and keep his commandments" (12:13). Pessimistic Qoheleth would say that this summary profoundly misunderstands the book. Carol Newsom calls it "Qoheleth's first mis-reading."[12] But is it a misreading? Admonitions to fear God and defenses of strict orthodox piety appear frequently in the book. Those earlier verses support the assertion in the epilogue and reflect its values. Fear God Qoheleth does not believe that all life is *hebel*. He trusted in divine power and divine presence to inflict harm on evildoers. He believed that fear of God and obedience based on that fear will have a positive effect.

Fear God Qoheleth believes that God governs the world justly and will judge the earth. In 5:6 he says, regarding foolish vows, "Why should God be angry at your words, and destroy the work of your hands?" God will punish the one who makes a thoughtless vow. And in 8:13 he says, "it will not be well with the wicked." In 11:9 he concludes, "For all these things God will bring you to judgment."

For Fear God Qoheleth, God orders the universe, punishing the wicked and (as we shall see) rewarding the righteous, those who fear God. Fear God Qoheleth says:

> With many dreams come varieties and a multitude of words; *but fear God.* (5:7)
> . . . for the one who *fears God* shall succeed. (7:18)

---

12. Carol A. Newsom, "Job and Ecclesiastes," in *Old Testament Interpretation: Past, Present, and Future: Essays in Honor of Gene M. Tucker,* ed. James Luther Mays, David L. Petersen, and Kent Harold Richards (Nashville: Abingdon, 1995), 189.

Yet I know that it will be well with those who *fear God.* (8:12)[13]

The author of the epilogue claims to have the key to understanding all of Qoheleth's writing. He identifies his words in chapter 12 as "the end of the matter," the final determinative say. The summation of Qoheleth's message is, "Fear God, and keep his commandments." The epilogue then ends with a warning of sure coming judgment: "For God will bring every deed into judgment, including every secret thing, whether good or evil."

It is often noted that "fear God" in Qoheleth does not have the generic meaning of "religion" or "piety" that it has in many other parts of the Bible. Rather, Fear God Qoheleth was afraid that God, a hostile divine being, would attack him. Note the following comments from various scholars: James Crenshaw says, "The fear of God comes very close to terror before an unpredictable despot."[14] Fox says, "Qohelet fears God, certainly but without warmth or fellowship."[15] Again, Crenshaw: "Qohelet's view of the deity lacks the warmth of the trusting relationship in some parts of the Hebrew Bible."[16] O. S. Rankin comments, "For Koheleth a man who fears God is a man who applies 'caution not to irritate this amoral Personality.'"[17] Robert Henry Pfeiffer says, "His activity discloses no traces of justice, mercy, or even of wisdom,"[18] and continues, "God proceeds deliberately and capriciously with the purpose of bewildering and mystifying the generations of men."[19] And finally, from William H. U. Anderson: "Here we are approaching the demonic."[20]

Timothy Polk takes a different view. He combines the voices of Fear God Qoheleth and Pessimistic Qoheleth and claims the entire book of Ecclesiastes is *about* the fear of God. He says, "Qoheleth seeks to disabuse us of

13. "These sentences sound so orthodox that commentators often seek to ascribe them, or the opinion expressed in them, to someone else. [Robert] Gordis reads them as quotations of conventional wisdom, which Qohelet repudiates. . . . But Qohelet states these principles as something *he* knows, as a fact rather than an opinion of which he is aware" (Michael V. Fox, *A Time to Tear Down and a Time to Build Up: A Rereading of Ecclesiastes* (Grand Rapids: Eerdmans, 1999), 56.

14. James L. Crenshaw, *Ecclesiastes* (OTL; Philadelphia: Westminster, 1987), 99-100.

15. Fox, *A Time to Tear Down,* 136-37.

16. Crenshaw, *Ecclesiastes,* 73.

17. O. S. Rankin, "The Book of Ecclesiastes," in *IB,* 5 (1956), 66-67.

18. Robert Henry Pfeiffer, "The Peculiar Skepticism of Ecclesiastes," *JBL* 53 (1934): 101.

19. Pfeiffer, "The Peculiar Skepticism of Ecclesiastes," 103.

20. Anderson, *Qoheleth and Its Pessimistic Theology,* 98ff.

all our delusion in order to bring us to the fear of God that we may experience joy."[21] Fox agrees, observing, "The book now says, even if everything is absurd, *nevertheless* we must fear God and keep his commandments."[22]

However, these quoted lines from Fear God Qoheleth assume a future judgment, probably an eschatological one. The people who fear God will succeed ultimately. In contrast, Pessimistic Qoheleth claimed that there is no relationship between what people do and their fate or destiny.

The Third Voice: Enjoy Life Qoheleth

In 1982 Norman Whybray published an article in which he surprised everyone by calling Qoheleth a "preacher of Joy."[23] He claimed that Qoheleth has been profoundly misunderstood by the critics. The negative statements had been taken out of context, he said, and in fact Qoheleth teaches that life is good and to be enjoyed with gusto — that the book of Ecclesiastes is not a pessimistic book at all, but rather upbeat. Attend to these lines. They appear to be from a different book entirely:

> There is nothing better for mortals than to eat and drink, and find enjoyment in their toil. (2:24)

> I know that there is nothing better for them than to be happy and enjoy themselves. (3:12)

> This is what I have seen to be good: it is fitting to eat and drink and find enjoyment in all the toil." (5:18)

> So I commend enjoyment, for there is nothing better for people under the sun than to eat, and drink, and enjoy themselves. (8:15)

> Go, eat your bread with enjoyment and drink your wine with a merry heart . . . Enjoy life with the wife whom you love. (9:7, 9)

> Light is sweet, and it is pleasant for the eyes to see the sun. (11:7)

21. Polk, "The Wisdom of Irony," 15.
22. Fox, *A Time to Tear Down*, 144.
23. R. N. Whybray, "Qoheleth, Preacher of Joy," *JSOT* 23 (1982): 87-98.

This voice commends enjoyment of life, which is a gift from God, and in fact, God commands people to have fun. This dramatically contrasts with the message of Pessimistic Qoheleth, who found pleasure to be *hebel*. Enjoy Life Qoheleth's voice is happy and positive, and this Qoheleth's God is open-handed and approachable.

These positive sentiments occur frequently in many different contexts in the book of Ecclesiastes. They say that life is good and that the physical and emotional pleasures of life are a great good. God gives them to humans as a generous gift, and God commands enjoyment. As if to underscore the importance of these moments, God is mentioned in connection with all but one of these passages:

This also, I saw, is from the hand of God. (2:24)
It is God's gift that all should eat and drink. (3:13)
For God has long ago approved what you do. (9:7)

There are three ways interpreters have understood the pleasure passages: First, some say that they are the actual advice from the author of the book, that one should take pleasure and enjoy life and the things it provides. In the light of the limitations of human understanding, taking pleasure in one's food and drink, one's companions, the beauties of nature and getting up every morning — these are a great good and a gift from God.

Alternatively, some have read the pleasure passages this way: Because of the realities of injustice and death, there are very few things that life has to offer. Considering the hunger and ignorance with which humans face life, this paltry little bit of fleeting pleasure is all that life has to offer, and we had better take it and squeeze all the juice out of it we can, because it's all we get, and we don't know for how long.

Or finally, some read the positive passages this way: The exhortations to pleasure are a mockery, because in the light of how fleeting and unjust life is, this pleasure will never make up for the human suffering and the desolation of death.[24]

---

24. "We thus, again, have two theories of pleasure: one that regards eating and drinking as a *faute de mieux* (2:24), and one that views pleasure as a gift of God. According to the first view, this kind of *simḥah*, viewed as purely temporary, is based on despair over our mortality"; T. A. Perry, *Dialogues With Kohelet: The Book Of Ecclesiastes* (University Park: Pennsylvania State University Press, 1993), 31. The exhortations to pleasure are localized advice that did not deflect the overall thesis that all is *hebel*. "Presumably, the little joys available to hu-

Considering the Voices Together

Does Qoheleth give us any hints about how to fit the book into a single structural or thematic whole? This has been a chief concern of most interpreters of Qoheleth. Crenshaw astutely observed, "Unless I am mistaken the essential issue for more than fifty years has been the search for an adequate means of explaining inconsistencies within the book."[25] Articles and commentaries give most of their energy and attention to "the contradictions" (what Crenshaw calls "inconsistencies"). He says:

> We hear Qoheleth admonish us to enjoy youth *for* we grow old; to enjoy toil *yet* it is a sorry business; to enjoy the *woman* whom we love *but* there is not one in a thousand(!); to eat, drink, and wear festive garments *yet* sorrow, fasting, and mourning are better; to pursue knowledge *but* it only increases sorrow; to embrace life, *yet* like the sword of Damocles the ancient sentence, "You must die," hangs over us.[26]

Benjamin Lyle Berger observes, "Some scholars have taken the contradictions in the book of Qohelet as an opportunity to flex their exegetical muscles either by forcing all contradictions into tenuous union or simply carving up the text."[27] Rather than "contradictions," I refer to the three voices. When two of the voices speak differently on the same topic, those are where we locate the contradictions.

The book itself gives scant information as to how the different voices should relate to each other. They have no transitional sentences between them, no discernible order. However, they cannot be separated. Frequently

---

mans merely made an otherwise intolerable situation bearable"; James L. Crenshaw, "Ecclesiastes, Book of," *ABD* 2 (1992), 277. "These are not solutions but *accommodations*. The answers come down to embracing the very activities that elsewhere he calls senseless: work and pleasure, wisdom and righteousness. These things are allowed value for the moment only. They allow humans to find good things — *little meanings* — within the vast absurd"; Fox, *A Time to Tear Down*, 140. "It more often than not seems to be either as a failed *hebel* plan for meaning and happiness in life, or as a concession and relief from the stress of his pessimistic view of the way the world works."

25. James L. Crenshaw, "Qoheleth in Current Research," *HAR* 7 (1983): 43, 45.
26. James L. Crenshaw, "The Eternal Gospel (Ecclesiastes 3:11)," in *Urgent Advice and Probing Questions: Collected Writings on Old Testament Wisdom* (Macon: Mercer University Press, 1995), 570.
27. Berger, "Qohelet and the Exigencies of the Absurd," 161, 163.

the same passage will serve different purposes for different voices. It is like conjoined twins who cannot be separated because they have too many points of attachment and share too many organs.

So for instance, the famous poem which begins, "For every thing there is a season" (3:1), for Enjoy Life Qoheleth is a celebration of the bounty of God's timely gifts. For Fear God Qoheleth, it is a sign of God's just governance of the world. For Pessimistic Qoheleth, it is a sign of God's indifference and inscrutability. Or consider this text, which gives me whiplash every time I read it:

> Rejoice, young man, while you are young, and let your heart cheer you in the days of your youth. Follow the inclination of your heart and the desire of your eyes. (11:9)

I would easily identify this text as Enjoy Life Qoheleth. But here is the whole verse with the last phrase included:

> Rejoice, young man, while you are young, and let your heart cheer you in the days of your youth. Follow the inclination of your heart and the desire of your eyes, *but know that for all these things God will bring you into judgment.* (Whiplash!)

God wants people to have fun in everything they do. But God will inflict punishment for every bit of it.

When one reads the book of Ecclesiastes, the three voices contend for dominance. Pessimistic Qoheleth and Fear God Qoheleth both have their own conclusion in which they tell the reader what it *all* finally means. The Pessimist declares (as he did at the beginning) that all is *hebel, hebel* to the highest degree. Fear God Qoheleth insists that the end of the matter is to fear God, obey the commandments. Enjoy Life Qoheleth has no summative conclusion.

Here follows a survey of reading strategies. Many have attributed the competing voices to multiple authors. Inevitably, the critics then choose one voice and ignore or marginalize the other two. The interpreter determines that a certain style or a certain theological assertion comes from the "authentic" Qoheleth and declares that any passages that say something different are by definition alien to the body of the text. A variant on this position states that a pious editor made the additions as means to render the book more orthodox. For instance, many interpreters insist that the epilogue is written by a pious editor who wanted to soften the transgressive nature of Pessimistic Qoheleth's opinions.

Some claim that the contrary passages, those determined to be not what Qoheleth believed, are deliberate foils for Qoheleth's argument. They are fictional interlocutors, written to set out and emphasize the strength of Qoheleth's arguments.[28] So these interpreters regard that Enjoy Life Qoheleth's hopefulness only exists to be smashed by the pessimistic argument. Alternatively, a few have argued that the author portrays Pessimistic Qoheleth as a bad example, proving the only alternative that all must fear God.[29] Others offer a psychological explanation for the different voices. The contradictions are understood as conflicts taking place within the psyche of the unitary author. This means that Qoheleth was a moody fellow, and the strongly negative passages (which I have identified as the pessimistic voice) belong to Qoheleth when he feels "down."[30] Some argue that Qoheleth's thoughts change over time. He moves from pessimism to optimism and faith in the course of the book. The contradictions of Qoheleth (they say) represent the conflicts within Qoheleth's mind as he faces the ambiguities of life. They reflect his confusion over these questions.[31] Finally, some claim that Ecclesiastes is a multivocal text. The three voices communicate what the author (or authors, or authors and editors) could not communicate using only one voice. Rather, they needed the confluence of tones and opinions. The presence of multiple voices reflects fundamental ambiguity on questions pertaining to the meaning of life.

Newsom observes that Ecclesiastes has no discernible structure, and that the meaning of many passages remains difficult and controversial and the most absolutely central words (such as *hebel*) cannot be reliably defined or definitively translated. She asserts "that it is the *nature* of Qoheleth to have these ambiguities." She goes on to say:

---

28. Michael V. Fox, "The Inner Structure of Qohelet's Thought," in *Qohelet in the Context of Wisdom,* ed. Antoon Schoors (BETL 136; Leuven: Leuven University Press and Peeters, 1998), 226.

29. Fox, *Qohelet and His Contradictions* (JSOTSup 71; Decatur: Almond, 1989), 26; Berger, "Qohelet and the Exigencies of the Absurd," 166, note 54.

30. See Fox, *A Time to Tear Down,* 90, note 3.

31. Polk, "The Wisdom of Irony," 15.

it is perhaps no accident that the book eludes the attempts of interpretive activity to fix its meaning determinately. I think that scholars have underestimated the significance of interpretive ambiguity in Ecclesiastes by seeing it as merely a problem to be solved. Perhaps it should be seen instead as another means of communicating the book's message.[32]

Berger observes, "The book of Qohelet is so consistently contradictory, so flawlessly difficult, that one is pushed to entertain the possibility that this medium of paradox was the intended stylistic carriage for the thought of the book. . . . In the end, it is this powerful effect of contradiction in the book of Qohelet that carries the book's message."[33] Brown comments, "Qoheleth's contradictions at the very least, seem to serve the didactic purpose of subverting facile interpretations of his discourse and heightening the larger ambiguity that engulfs the book."[34] Fox notes the existence of "two equally valid but contradictory principles. [Qoheleth] does not resolve these antinomies, but only describes them, bemoans them, and suggests how to live in such a refractory world."[35]

It would be tempting to stop here, to see these three voices as three parts to a whole, working in concert — that one must hear all three voices in order to truly understand the book. But no — the book of Ecclesiastes is at war within itself, a war in which a reader must take sides; in which, as I mentioned earlier, I must take sides.

The Pessimistic Qoheleth Is the True Voice of the Book

There are two reasons why, in a multivocal text such as this, I might advocate one reading over another. The first is if the weight of literary evidence leads one to conclude that a single voice dominates. Second, I must consider the ethical dimension of this interpretive decision. Interpretations have consequences in the real world, and interpreters must take responsibility for the effects of one's interpretation.

32. Newsom, "Job and Ecclesiastes," 190.

33. Berger, "Qohelet and the Exigencies of the Absurd," 161, 163.

34. William P. Brown, *Ecclesiastes* (Interpretation; Louisville: Westminster John Knox, 2011), 12.

35. Fox, *A Time to Tear Down*, 3, 68; see Anderson, *Qoheleth and Its Pessimistic Theology*, 73.

The structural argument has already been made for preferring Pessimistic Qoheleth. We have the same sweeping, general statement at the beginning and the end of the corpus: "All is *hebel.*" The one who wields this frame is the one who controls the book. Further, in the inside of this frame, "vanity" echoes at key moments throughout. When I first read the book and encountered the three voices, I had unconsciously decided to listen to only the one. I came to an agreement with Pessimistic Qoheleth to read the book his way, which means, in a sense, I agreed to read the book carelessly, skipping over the other two voices. So now I bring the other two voices back into the discussion.

Perhaps the best way to frame the question would be to ask, which of the three Qoheleths would I want to be my teacher? I would never want Fear God Qoheleth as a guide. I realize that the concept of the fear of Yahweh has a long, complex, and not negative pedigree within the Hebrew Bible. Nevertheless, Fear God Qoheleth's piety is too severe and demanding. Moreover, what he writes smacks of sloganeering and talking points. His spirituality is shallow, unrealistic, and authoritarian. I don't trust him. I don't respect him.

Enjoy Life Qoheleth is a more difficult case. I like him very much, and enjoy having him around. But honestly, he is a little flighty and superficial. I'm not sure he would be good in an emergency. "How is enjoyment to be considered 'meaning' in life?" Anderson asks. "Is this not a rather superficial and highly materialistically based presumption?"[36] Carolyn Sharp adds, "Qohelet's rhetorical grasping for joy is a desperate, unconvincing paraenesis that serves only to highlight how distanced his (constructed) reality is from the desired fruits of his lifelong search for wisdom."[37]

No. I choose Pessimistic Qoheleth. I begin to realize he's the one I trusted all along. He makes problematic the question of meaning; by that I mean that he takes these questions out of dogmatic categories and thus disturbs settled opinion. He slips in his own position, forcefully, but allows other voices to be heard. Its author speaks in anguish about the intractable mystery of existence. One alternative voice speaks in glowing terms about the possibilities of life, and a third voice closes the book with a pious expla-

36. William H. U. Anderson, "Ironic Correlations and Scepticism in the Joy Statements of Qoheleth," *SJOT* 14 (2000): 93.

37. Carolyn J. Sharp, "Ironic Representation, Authorial Voice, and Meaning in Qohelet," *BibInt* 12 (2004): 59. Cf. Anderson, "Ironic Correlations and Scepticism," 96-97.

nation. Where these three voices meet, there are contradictions. These contradictions lie at the heart of the book. They are its most important feature.

I cannot claim that one voice has superior literary quality, because the different voices cannot be separated, laid side by side, and compared. I cannot say that one argument is superior, because the superior argument would only be the one I find most convincing. Claims to authenticity tend to be circular: one decides the most authentic voice and then grants that voice authority by virtue of its authenticity. But I argue that by "authentic voice of Qoheleth" I mean the best voice, the wisest voice, the voice I most want people to listen to, the one that makes the most unique contribution to the tradition, that has the most integrity, the voice with humor and irony, the one most fully human. One finishes reading Ecclesiastes (I claim), not thinking "fear God," not thinking "life is great," but rather, "vanity of vanities!"

QUESTIONS FOR REVIEW

Q What are the three voices in the book of Ecclesiastes?

Q What are the various ways to understand the "pleasure passages" in Ecclesiastes?

Q Why does Penchansky argue that the pessimistic voice is the true voice of Ecclesiastes?

KEY WORDS

– *Hebel,* vanity

– "fear God"

FOR FURTHER READING

Crenshaw, James L. *A Whirlpool of Torment: Israelite Traditions of God as an Oppressive Presence.* OBT 12. Philadelphia: Fortress, 1984.

Fox, Michael V. *A Time to Tear Down and a Time to Build Up: A Rereading of Ecclesiastes.* Grand Rapids: Eerdmans, 1999.

5. Sounds of Silence: The *Absence* of Covenantal Theology in the Wisdom Literature

I will show you; listen to me; what I have seen I will declare — what sages have told, and their ancestors have not hidden, to whom alone the land was given, and no stranger passed among them.

JOB 15:17-19

Who can say, "I have made my heart clean, I am pure from my sin"?

PROVERBS 20:9

I have made a covenant with my eyes; how then could I look upon a virgin?

JOB 31:1

[She] forsakes the partner of her youth and forgets her sacred covenant.

PROVERBS 2:17

Surprisingly, the books of Proverbs, Job, and Ecclesiastes lack reference to Israelite covenants.[1] In other biblical books, Yahweh makes covenants with the ancestors, Abraham and Jacob. He makes a covenant with

---

1. There is one notable exception in Job. See below for discussion on that verse.

the Israelites under Moses' leadership and another covenant with King David and his progeny. These covenants motivate and energize most of the Hebrew Bible, the later Jewish books, the rabbinical writings, and the New Testament. How then can we account for the silence of these first three wisdom books (Proverbs, Job, Ecclesiastes) regarding what seems central for the other parts of the Bible?

The later wisdom books, Sirach and the Wisdom of Solomon, refer to the covenants copiously. For instance, Sirach assures his readers, "All this is the book of the covenant of the Most High God, the law that Moses commanded us" (Sir 24:23).[2] Something changed in this period to occasion the addition of this content (the Israelite covenants). This change altered the content and concerns of wisdom literature. With the imposition of Hellenistic culture, the sages now speak freely of Abraham, Moses, and David. They refer to the covenants and consider themselves participants in Israel's covenantal relationship with Yahweh.

The first three books (Job, Proverbs, and Ecclesiastes) scarcely mention covenant or covenantal themes. The second two mention Israelite covenants frequently. Why the difference? What changed was that Alexander the Great conquered the Middle East and imposed Greek (Hellenistic) culture upon the region. The Greek wisdom books were significantly influenced by Hellenistic culture. They brought Israelite covenantal ideas into wisdom writings.

The Israelite Covenants

People in the ancient Near East believed that the gods made covenants with individuals and with nations. In the biblical tradition, Yahweh makes certain covenants exclusively with the Israelite/Judean communities. Israelites write accounts about when the covenants were first made. These founding stories give these communities a sense of meaning and destiny. The three covenants that specifically single out the Israelite and Judean communities are: (1) The covenant that Yahweh makes with the ancestors beginning with Abraham. By means of this covenant relationship, Yahweh

2. Wis 9:8; 10:15-21; 11 (whole chapter); 18 (whole chapter); 19 (whole chapter); Sir 3:2-16; 16:8-10; 17:1, 17; 23:12 "inheritance of Jacob"; 24 (whole chapter); wisdom in temple, 24:23; 28:7; 35:1, 5; 39:1; 42:2; 44–50 (famous men).

gives the land of Canaan to Abraham's descendants (Genesis 12–50). He passes on this covenant to his son Isaac, and so on. The Israelite and Judean people inherited this relationship and these promises, and they believed that it gave them rights to the land and that it showed the special preferential relationship between Yahweh and these people. (2) The Sinai covenant — Israel, now a nation and a numerous people, makes a covenant with Yahweh in the wilderness. It establishes a relationship between Yahweh and the people with obligations for both signatories. (3) The Davidic covenant — the name given to the cluster of agreements Yahweh made with the family of David, whereby Yahweh assured that David's family would always maintain control over the Israelite territory and people.

These three covenants in most ways determine the religious identity of ancient Israel and the entities that sprung from it (the smaller nations of Israel and Judah, the returning exiles in the Persian colony of Yehud, and finally, the Jews and the Christians). I shall refer collectively to these three covenants as "the Israelite Covenants."

The Silence

Each of these three books, Job, Proverbs, and Ecclesiastes, has had many authors and even more editors. That no one in this relatively large group saw fit to insert covenantal language into the material suggests a commonality of purpose and vision. The group of individuals responsible for Job, for the various "books" of Proverbs, and the multiple editorial layers of Qoheleth each shared this perspective, whatever it is, that led them to exclude this material. It affected them all equally, over time.

When I claim that these three books of Hebrew wisdom lack reference to Israelite covenant, what exactly do they lack? What is it we are looking for but do not find? When one reads the Hebrew wisdom books, certain items are notable in their absence when compared to other books of the Bible, and more specifically when compared with the Greek wisdom books. What they lack are exactly those things which one associates with the Israelite covenants. Ordinarily we dismiss "arguments from silence" as spurious and suspect. But in the Hebrew Bible there are many silences that cry out for interpretation. How we interpret these silences, how we fill them in, determines how we read these stories. I will examine five different areas by means of which one would determine the presence of covenantal themes:

1. Concepts closely connected with covenant ideas or covenant texts, references to exodus events, ancestral covenants, or the covenant Yahweh made with King David.
2. Key words — names of the ancestors, references to the land of Israel, Canaan, Sinai or Horeb (alternate names for the mountain where Moses received the law), Covenant (Hebrew *Berît*), *ḥesed*, which may be translated "covenant love" or "covenant faithfulness," Sea of Reeds, Pharaoh, Egypt, David, etc.
3. References to religious practices that are related to the covenant prescriptions in the Torah (the first five books). This would include references to specific animal sacrifices or dietary prohibitions.
4. Ethical references — any that are specific to the Torah.
5. Literary dependence on other indisputably covenantal books, Jeremiah or Genesis, for instance.

Concepts

Normally, at this point in the chapter I would be giving examples, but there are none. There is silence. None of those five items are found in the first three wisdom books. However, some come close to covenant ideas, and I examine them here. These are concepts in Hebrew wisdom books that resemble ideas one finds in other parts of the Bible:

Fear of God The phrase "fear of God" appears frequently in Hebrew wisdom books. One finds in the first book of Proverbs, for instance,[3] "the fear of Yahweh is the beginning of knowledge" (Prov 1:7). In the book of Job, the narrator describes Job as one who "feared God and turned away from evil" (Job 1:1b). One of the strongest admonitions in the book of Ecclesiastes is to "fear God": ". . . for the one who *fears God* shall succeed" (Eccl 7:18). "Yet I know it will be well with those who *fear God*" (8:12). This notion of fearing God is a common phrase throughout the Hebrew Bible. For instance, one reads in Gen 42:18 that Joseph says to his brothers, "Do this and you will live, for I fear God." In Exod 18:21, Moses' father-in-law advises him, "You should also look for able men

3. The book of Proverbs divides easily into a number of books, most with a definite introduction and conclusion.

among all the people, men who fear God, are trustworthy. . . ." In Psalms, one reads, "Come and hear, all you who fear God, and I will tell what he has done for me" (Ps 66:16).

Yahweh The name Yahweh was the name of choice when referring to the Israelite God in much of Job and Proverbs. The book of Ecclesiastes does not use the name at all. Some might claim that Yahweh serves as a covenant name, and its use in Job and Proverbs connects this material with Israelite covenants. In Exodus, the name is linked with the Israelite covenant. "'Thus you shall say to the Israelites, 'Yahweh, the God of your ancestors, the God of Abraham, the God of Isaac, and the God of Jacob, has sent me to you': This is my name forever, and this my title for all generations" (Exod 3:15). There is no consistency in the usage of this special name, either in wisdom books or in the rest of the Bible. Yahweh is used both in Hebrew wisdom books and elsewhere in the Bible, and as in Ecclesiastes, in some other parts of the Bible the name does not occur. Therefore, one finds no direct relationship between the use of the name Yahweh and Israelite covenant ideas. The sages were Yahwists. But they were Yahwists of a different sort, who defined differently their sacred connections with Yahweh. They did not use any of the Israelite covenant stories to express their Yahwism or to bolster their arguments.[4]

Creation There are two creation accounts in Genesis, which represent two different traditions. Similarly, there are creation accounts in the Hebrew wisdom books. In Proverbs, for instance, Yahweh creates the primal landscape. Lady Wisdom, as a young child, looks on: "Before the mountains had been shaped, before the hills, I was brought forth. . . . When he established the heavens, I was there, when he drew a circle on the face of the deep . . ." (Prov 8:25, 27).

In Job, Yahweh's speeches provide a glimpse into the first moments of creation, when "the morning stars sang together and all the heavenly beings shouted for joy" (Job 38:4-7). In Ecclesiastes, Qoheleth enjoins his readers to enjoy God's creation: "There is nothing better for mortals than

---

4. It is possible that the use of the term Yahweh in the early sapiential literature is without reflection, simply meaning "deity"; J. Coert Rylaarsdam, *Revelation in Jewish Wisdom Literature* (Chicago: University of Chicago Press, 1946), 21. I maintain rather that the name is characteristically Israelite, but not necessarily connected to any Israelite covenant.

to eat and drink, and find enjoyment in their toil" (Eccl 2:24). In his own way, Qoheleth makes his case for the goodness of creation.

That there is a wisdom theology of creation there can be no doubt. A theology of creation plays an important role in how the sages situate themselves in the world. However, there are different theologies of creation within the Hebrew Bible. The tradition behind the Genesis 1 account sees creation as the imposition of order and duality upon a chaotic disorderly universe. The tradition behind Genesis 2 understood creation as a hierarchy in which were established strict moral boundaries as a result of the failed human experiment in the garden of Eden.

One might argue that the existence of creation stories in both Genesis and Hebrew wisdom books is an argument for the close connection and shared perspective of these parts of the Bible. This is how it is reasoned. The Genesis creation stories are reflected in Exodus (the Israelite covenant document). The parting of the sea reflects how God in Genesis 1 separates the waters above and below the great vault of heaven. Both mention a seven-day rest. Therefore, the wisdom books that speak of creation must also be linked to Exodus. However, the references to creation in Wisdom do not mention the seventh day Sabbath rest, as does Genesis 2.

Many texts in the Hebrew wisdom books speak of the mystery of creation. "But where shall wisdom be found? And where is the place of understanding? Mortals do not know the way to it, and it is not found in the land of the living" (Job 28:12-13). Other Hebrew sages represent the predictability of creation. Each of these Hebrew wisdom creation theologies ill fits the picture of the Genesis creation accounts. In different ways Job and Proverbs question that predictability of the created order, and the book of Ecclesiastes denies it altogether.

Retribution The sapiential picture of retribution has similarities to the one put forth by the Deuteronomic History. This is a term used to describe the books Joshua, Judges, 1 and 2 Samuel, 1 and 2 Kings. They share (it is said) a common perspective that they derive from the book of Deuteronomy. When Israel and its kings obeyed Yahweh, they succeeded. When they worshipped other gods, they failed and God destroyed them. This is retribution.

However, whereas the Deuteronomist refers to the entire nation, in wisdom the individual is emphasized. Although there is some similarity, the two theological schools must be understood as creating entirely different worlds. Wisdom's law of retribution is different from what one finds in Deuteronomic History, where the consequences are meted out to nations and their representative monarchs. In the wisdom books they are meted out to individuals. In the Deuteronomic History, there is a set structure of sin resulting in punishment. In Hebrew wisdom there is a similar structure of reward and punishment. However, in Deuteronomy and its progeny the punishment is based on violations of the covenant.[5] The Deuteronomic retribution is corporate, that is, it concerns entire nations. For the sages, retribution is primarily visited upon an individual. The idea that gods punish humans for sin is common in ancient literature and is not a characteristic that distinguishes the Israelite covenant literature from other literature.

Boundary Keeping Deuteronomy commands that the ancient boundary stones not be moved. "You must not move your neighbor's boundary marker, set up by former generations, on the property that will be allotted to you in the land that Yahweh your God is giving you to possess" (Deut 19:14; also 27:17). Both the books of Proverbs and Job speak similarly about boundary stones.[6] Raymond Van Leeuwen claims that this similarity is evidence of a strong connection between the Torah and the Hebrew wisdom books.[7]

Use of the Word "Covenant" The word "covenant" occurs occasionally in the first three wisdom books. However, most of the examples refer to the original meaning of the term — an agreement between two parties for the purpose of cessation of hostility and mutual benefit.[8] Both the sages and the Israelite majority employed this notion freely. They applied it differ-

---

5. Both traditions have countertraditions that argue against the adequacy of the retribution structure.

6. "Yahweh will tear down the house of the proud,/but he will establish the homestead of the widow" (Prov 15:25). "Do not remove the ancient boundary stone/that your ancestors set up" (22:28). "Do not remove ancient boundary stones" (23:10).

7. This "presupposes the historical tradition of the giving of the land. For at that time, Yahweh established boundaries which remained the basis for justice throughout Israel's history (Job 15:18-19)"; Raymond C. Van Leeuwen, "The Book of Proverbs," in *The New Interpreter's Bible*, ed. Leander E. Keck (Nashville: Abingdon, 2005), 122.

8. Francis Brown, S. R. Driver, and Charles A. Briggs, *A Hebrew and Aramaic Lexicon of the Old Testament* (rev. ed.; Oxford: Oxford University Press, 1953), 136.

ently, however. Proverbs 2:17, for example, speaks of a woman "forsaking the covenant of her God." Might that be a reference to the Sinai covenant? Probably not. Covenants between gods and humans are not limited to Sinai. This general reference does not allude to a specific national covenant.

Land Given to the "Fathers" I searched far and wide to find a single instance where a Hebrew wisdom book mentioned explicitly something from one of the Israelite covenants. There is only one, and it is a special case.[9] Job 15:17-19 says:

> I will show you; listen to me; what I have seen I will declare — what sages have told, and their ancestors have not hidden, to whom alone the land was given, and no stranger passed among them.

This refers to an Israelite covenant and not to some random deal for land. It speaks of an ancient tradition passed down three times: (1) "What *I* have seen" — the sage who wrote these lines; (2) "what *sages* have told" — those who taught the sage who wrote these lines; (3) "what *ancestors* have not hidden" — distant ancestors who passed this on to the earliest sages. "Ancestors" might refer to generic forerunners, but more likely it refers to "the ancestors," that is, the founding patriarchs of the Israelite tradition, Abraham, Isaac, and Jacob, to whom God promised "the land."

The coupling of "ancestors" with "land" suggests strongly the stories that connect the Israelites with the land, stories now found in Genesis 12–36. Eliphaz refers to the past event wherein Yahweh gave the land (Palestine) to the Fathers. In Genesis it says, "Then the LORD appeared to Abram, and said, 'To your offspring I will give this land'" (Gen 12:7). According to Eliphaz, the sages (the *hakamim*) became the guardians of the traditions, specifically the narrative account of how Yahweh gave the land (Palestine) to the "ancestors." This passage combines the ideas of tradition, ancestors, and land, a potent covenantal combination.

Eliphaz refers to the Israelite covenant that God made with Abraham. In what context does this statement appear and who says it? How does the

---

9. Marvin H. Pope, *Job* (AB 15; Garden City: Doubleday, 1973), 116; David J. A. Clines, "Why Is There a Book of Job and What Does It Do to You If You Read It?" in *The Book of Job*, ed. W. A. M. Beuken (Leuven: Leuven University Press, 1994), 1-20; Norman C. Habel, *The Book of Job* (London: Cambridge University Press, 1975), 258.

author regard this Israelite covenant? Eliphaz, one of Job's three "friends," comes to "comfort" him. In reality, they seek to support their own theological position at their friend Job's expense. He must be proven wrong and sinful so they can feel safe — that what happened to Job (a sinner) would never happen to righteous people like them. Before looking any further, we might say that Eliphaz is not a reliable source. But there is more.

The context of the quotation enables one to understand its significance. Eliphaz argues most strongly for traditional Israelite values. He describes "the gray-haired and the aged" as "on our side" (Job 15:10). Eliphaz uses these authorities (and the "ancestors" a few verses later) in order to give credence to his assertion that the wicked are always and invariably punished.

How then must one regard this offhand comment about the tradition passed down that the land was given to the ancestors? The author of Job regarded the advice and theological insights of the three friends as worthless. In 42:7 it says, "After the Lord had spoken these words to Job, the Lord said to Eliphaz the Temanite: 'My wrath is kindled against you and against your two friends; for you have not spoken of me what is right, as my servant Job has.'" Note that what Eliphaz and his two friends have said *is not right* (or true), and that God is angry with Eliphaz because of what he has said. On an entirely different level, then, Eliphaz is an unreliable witness.

By mentioning the Israelite covenant (unheard of and unexpected within wisdom circles), and by placing it in the mouth of the repudiated Eliphaz, the writer shows at best his indifference and at worst his contempt for the ancestral stories. The Israelite covenant would then have as much value as any of the other specious (and wrath-inducing) arguments raised by the friends.

In Job, the covenant idea is not important. This statement of Eliphaz is the only explicit mention of any of the Israelite covenants in any Hebrew wisdom book. Only one mention in three books (85 chapters total) is a notable absence.

Cultic References (Sacrifices, Vows, Prayer) The practices of the Israelite cult — sacrifices, rituals, holy days — are embedded in the covenant that God made with Moses in the books of the Torah (Exodus-Deuteronomy). There are references in the first three Hebrew wisdom books to religious rituals, particularly animal sacrifice. However, this was generally true for all ancient cultures and does not imply a specific connection to the Israelite covenant rituals.

Sacrifice and temple worship are common to Hebrew wisdom literature as well as other Hebrew literary traditions. Qoheleth gives advice about cultic behavior: "Guard your steps when you go to the house of God; to draw near to listen is better than the sacrifice offered by fools; for they do not know how to keep from doing evil" (Eccl 5:1). Like their neighbors and their families, their fellow-countrymen, fellow worshipers of Yahweh, the sages offered sacrifice, made vows, and attended temple ceremonies. These commonly held practices do not militate against the claim that sages maintained a distinct set of beliefs. In Hebrew wisdom are descriptions of general religious behavior or religious language with no specific connection with anything one finds characteristically in other biblical traditions.

Hebrew wisdom literature frequently mentions prayer: "O that I might have my request, and that God would grant my desire" (Job 6:8). However, the petitions are not based on one of the Israelite covenants. Contrast these examples from Psalms. In Psalm 105:42-43, the psalmist refers to the ancestral covenant: "For he remembered his holy promise, and Abraham, his servant. So he brought his people out with joy." In Psalm 89:49, the psalmist reminds Yahweh of his covenant: "Lord, where is your steadfast love of old, which by your faithfulness you swore to David?" There is nothing that corresponds to this in Hebrew wisdom.

Proverbs 20:9 declares: "Who can say, 'I have made my heart clean; I am pure from my sin'?" The sage asks a rhetorical question, expecting a negative answer. The author argues that no individual can be entirely pure. He speaks of the action of "cleansing the heart" and "purging sin." These are vague references to actions one might take to receive forgiveness or cleansing. The author never gets specific about which acts, whether animal sacrifice, ceremonial cleansing, or ritual might have accomplished the cleansing. In any case, according to this maxim, the efforts are (at best) ineffectual. There is no attention to activities specifically directed by the ritual portions of the Torah.

Job offered sacrifice on behalf of his children. Many have noted here a similarity to the religious practice of the ancestors — a patriarch who sacrifices on behalf of his family, functioning as priest. But when Job challenges the behavior of Yahweh, he does not appeal to one of the Israelite covenants (as do the psalmists). He appeals to his past experience with Yahweh, the traditional understanding that Yahweh is fair, and his innate sense of rightness.

Ethical References The Ten Commandments condense the ethical, cultural, and theological prescriptions of the Sinai covenant. Some of the commandments concern specifically the Israelites' relationship to Yahweh. They specify exclusive worship, forbid images, and enjoin Sabbath observance and respect for Yahweh's personal name by not using it in a curse formula. The remaining commandments deal with human relationships (do not steal; do not lie, etc.). The sages in their writings made frequent references to similar prescriptions.

The ninth commandment,[10] for instance, says, "You shall not bear false witness against your neighbor" (Exod 20:16). Similarly, in Proverbs it says, "Do not be a witness against your neighbor without cause, and do not deceive with your lips" (Prov 24:28). And again from Proverbs: "Like a war club, a sword, or a sharp arrow is one who bears false witness against a neighbor" (Prov 25:18). The law forbids adultery in the seventh commandment, and in Proverbs it says, "Can one walk on hot coals/without scorching the feet?/So is he who sleeps with his neighbor's wife;/no one who touches her will go unpunished" (Prov 6:28-29). The sixth commandment prohibits murder and the eighth, stealing, and both find a reflection in Proverbs 1:

10 My child, if sinners entice you,
   do not consent.
11 If they say, "Come with us, let us lie in wait for blood;
   let us wantonly ambush the innocent . . ."
15 my child, do not walk in their way,
   keep your foot from their paths.

Finally, many places in Proverbs urge one to honor father and mother, which is also the substance of the fifth commandment. In Prov 20:20, for example, we read, "If you curse father or mother, your lamp will go out in utter darkness." A different verse in Proverbs reflects the law against coveting (the tenth commandment): "Do not envy the wicked, nor desire to be with them" (24:1, 19).

The first four commandments are unmistakably left out of Proverbs, Job, and Ecclesiastes, except for a dim echo of the first commandment in Job 31:26-27. In Job's oath of innocence, he says: "If I have looked at the sun

10. Eighth in the Catholic numbering system.

when it shone, or the moon moving in splendor, and my heart has been secretly enticed, and my mouth has kissed my hand. . . ." In this verse Job swears that he did not worship the moon. Thus he implies that the worship of the moon is a bad thing, which might further imply that perhaps the worship of any god other than Yahweh is a bad thing. This might allude to the first commandment — "You shall have no other gods before me" (Exod 20:3). However, the distance is vast from not worshipping the moon to "you shall have no other gods before me." The second commandment (no idolatry), the third (respecting God's name), and the fourth commandment (honor the Sabbath) remain unmentioned in these three Hebrew wisdom books.

Key Words

There are certainly places in the Hebrew literature that contain words traditionally associated with Israelite covenant ideas. However, Proverbs, Job, and Qoheleth neither mention or allude to any of these words: Canaan, Sinai, Sea of Reeds. Nor is there mention in Hebrew wisdom of Abraham, Isaac, and Jacob. But Israel, David, and Solomon are mentioned in Prov 1:1, and Solomon alone is implied in Ecclesiastes (1:1, 12). Both these texts introduce Solomon as king over Israel, only to establish the writer's rhetorical authority — if Solomon wrote it, it had more authority.

Hesed in the Psalms and elsewhere refers to "God's covenant love," or "the faithful love that God expressed when God made a covenant with the people." Writers call on God's *hesed* to give them blessings: ". . . preserve my life according to your steadfast love *(hesed)*" (Ps 119:159). The same word occurs in Job and Proverbs, but in contexts that are not covenant-related. In Job 37:13 one reads, "Whether for correction, or for his land, or for love *(hesed)*, he causes it [the thunderstorm] to happen." Proverbs 11:17 says, "Those who are kind reward *(hesed)* themselves." In 14:22 we read, "Those who plan good find loyalty *(hesed)* and faithfulness." These texts in Proverbs and Job refer to love, but not to any particularly Israelite characteristic of covenant.

Horeb is not mentioned in the sapiential literature until Sirach.[11] This Greek wisdom book also says, "He allowed him to hear his voice, and led

11. "You heard rebuke at Sinai and judgments of vengeance at Horeb" (Sir 48:7).

him into the dark cloud, and gave him the commandments face to face, the law of life and knowledge, so that he might teach Jacob the covenant, and Israel his decrees" (Sir 45:5). Nothing close to that is in the Hebrew wisdom books.

Berît is usually translated as "covenant," or "testament. The occurrences of the word in Job and Proverbs prove nothing however, because they are general in their reference. They might be alluding to any covenant, and are not coupled with any specific Israelite reference. For example:

> For you shall be in league *(berît)* with the stones of the field, and the wild animals shall be at peace with you. (Job 5:23)

> I have made a covenant *(berît karati)* with my eyes; how then could I look upon a virgin? (Job 31:1)

> Will it (Leviathan) make a covenant *(hayikrot berît)* with you to be taken as your servant forever? (Job 41:4)

> [The forbidden woman] who forsakes the partner of her youth and forgets her sacred covenant *(berît).* (Prov 2:17)

In each case, one can note a similarity between something in the Hebrew wisdom books and covenant theology. The question is, are these similarities significant? I say no, for the following reasons. They lack some key details that (for example) would connect it with Israelite sacrifice (as opposed to generic, ancient Near Eastern sacrifice), details such as specific mention of covenant characters, allusions to specific Israelite laws (as opposed to generalized ethical concerns), and principles held by many.

Virtually all biblical scholars affirm the central importance of these covenants for understanding the ancient Israelite religion and its religious literature. This silence about them in the Hebrew wisdom books then makes a loud noise that demands attention. People decry arguments from silence because the silences may be filled in so many ways, and silence provides little check on the imagination. However, this silence must be explained. How do we account for the complete absence of covenantal words or concepts in these wisdom books?

I have assembled all the evidence I could find, or that I could devise, that might suggest that the Israelite covenants might pervade and underlie the Hebrew wisdom books. What I have found is that mostly there is no mention, no allusion to the Israelite covenants at all, except for one specific reference in Job to Yahweh's promise of land, put in the mouth of one of the story's negative, wrong-headed figures. I therefore conclude that the similarities are not significant in the determination of the sages' predisposition towards the Israelite covenants. I further conclude that the silence at the heart of wisdom literature, its lack of attention to Israelite covenants, is huge, is gaping, and fraught with significance.

Locating Underlying Scholarly Predispositions

Why do so many argue for a pervasive covenantal presence in all portions of Scripture? The importance some feel to include wisdom as part of a harmonious whole is part of the larger search in biblical scholarship for a ruling metaphor to unify the entire Bible. The emphasis on the covenant in Talmudic Judaism, the New Testament, and the history of the Christian communities leads many to look for evidence within the sacred text of a unified outlook that places Israelite covenants at the center.

Most deal with Hebrew wisdom in one of three ways, usually acknowledging the apparent absence of covenantal reference in these texts.[12] (1) They claim that the books are unabashedly covenantal, though in some hidden way.[13] I have demonstrated how this receives scant support from the Hebrew wisdom books. (2) They claim that the sages did not speak of the covenant because they were concerned with "other things" — practical wisdom, the natural order, the material world.[14] The international flavor of wisdom, while not reducing the sages' covenantal loyalty, precludes

12. Roland E. Murphy, *The Tree of Life: An Exploration of Biblical Wisdom Literature* (ABRL; 1st ed., New York: Doubleday, 1990), 1, 62, 113; Rylaarsdam, *Revelation in Jewish Wisdom Literature*, 20; Gerhard von Rad, *Old Testament Theology* (New York: Harper & Row), 1:412, 415, 439; Michael V. Fox, "Review of *Die Weisheit Israels*," *CBQ* 111 (1992): 135.

13. Rylaarsdam, *Revelation in Jewish Wisdom Literature*, 18; Donn F. Morgan, *Wisdom in the Old Testament Traditions* (Atlanta: John Knox, 1981), 143, 151; von Rad, *Old Testament Theology*, 1:433, 445; Van Leeuwen, "The Book of Proverbs," 122.

14. Rylaarsdam, *Revelation in Jewish Wisdom Literature*, 20, 26; H. Weeler Robinson, *Inspiration and Revelation in the Old Testament* (Oxford: Clarendon, 1946), 231; von Rad, *Old Testament Theology*, 1:433, 435, 452; Walther Eichrodt, *Theology of the Old Testament* (OTL; Philadelphia: Westminster, 1967), 2:81.

them speaking of the covenant. Such references, it was feared, might exclude their non-Israelite readers. The sages wanted their texts to pass international muster. (3) They ignore the sapiential material.[15]

The first contemporary scholars who studied wisdom regarded it as inferior to the rest of the Bible, less spiritual, more materialistic. Early writers about Hebrew wisdom saw the silence as an indication of wisdom's inferiority. They said that the writers of Hebrew wisdom concerned themselves with trivial things. Because they believed Solomon wrote Proverbs and Ecclesiastes, they pointed to Solomon's apostasy as reason enough for the "unspiritual tone" of the Hebrew wisdom writing. King Solomon at the height of his power married foreign woman and worshiped their gods (1 Kgs 11:1-13). Because these writings were deficient in the divine grace that comes with special revelation, Hebrew wisdom therefore was inferior. God did not appear to them upon a mountain or in a prophetic trance or vision. Gerhard von Rad tried to correct this disparagement of wisdom, arguing that wisdom served as the human response to the covenant.[16] He thus forced Hebrew wisdom into a role that ill fit.

Theories to Explain the Silence

I have explored the contours of the silence regarding the Israelite covenants. Now another question must be explored. The silence must be filled. It cries out for explanation. There are *four* possible ways to fill the silence. *First,* there are those who assert that the writers of Proverbs, Job, and Ecclesiastes believed in and participated in the covenantal theologies of the northern Israelite and southern Judean communities. However, they did not mention covenants in their works because their writings were concerned with other things. In this explanation, the sages shared a common religious sensibility with regard to the covenants. They assumed the existence of the covenants but did not need to telegraph that fact. This pre-

---

15. Those who hold that wisdom literature employs the covenant are prone to excessively pious statements. For instance, Franz-Josef Steiert assumes "the principle of monotheism in itself entails everything else in Israelite religion. . . . Indeed, God's name in itself contains 'das alttestamentlich Evangelium' [!] in nuce"; quoted in Fox, "Review of *Die Weisheit Israels*," 136.

16. Von Rad, *Old Testament Theology*, 1:77.

sumes that the importance and pervasiveness of the covenantal idea were held universally in ancient Israel.

In the *second* explanation, the sages opposed and rebelled against the three covenants. They did not mention them because they felt contempt for the covenantal ideas, particularly the intolerance and chauvinism of the exclusively Israelite laws contained in the covenant. They avoided mention of the covenant as a means to show their contempt for covenantal thinking. The *third* explanation varies slightly from the second. In this case, the sages were silent not out of protest, but rather out of fear. They feared that if they came out against the covenant idea they would be persecuted.

In the *fourth* explanation, the Hebrew sages did not mention the covenant because they regarded covenantal ideas as inconsequential and unimportant. This would presume the possibility of an Israelite in good standing who was scarcely aware of some other groups who believe a complicated array of ideas and laws (the Israelite covenants). These covenants would have little importance and relevance for the sages.

Silent but Sympathetic

In the first explanation the silence is incidental, because the subject of the covenants never came up. They were not speaking of covenants because they concerned themselves with more practical and worldly matters. I make my point more clearly when I present an imaginary sage, one who believed passionately in the Israelite covenants, but never mentioned them in any of his professional writings. In this I illustrate one way the silence might be explained:

> Yakov woke at six to attend morning prayers in the temple. He loved the smell of the incense and the intonation of the priest as he called the people to prayer. Yakov had spent the previous week in the Egyptian court as an emissary to the king, and how good it was to be home.
>
> As a king's diplomat, he spoke the ancient languages in a near perfect accent, and he had charmed his Egyptian counterparts with his knowledge of the ways of their kingdom and their traditional stories. He carefully concealed his contempt for their society, their smugness and superiority; even their clothing and dress revolted him. He knew from

his own sacred stories what Egypt had done to Israel in the past, and therefore he could not trust them. He never said what he thought, that Yahweh had destined Israel to rule the world. He never even let on that he knew this. He kept a professional silence.

Israel knew that God had chosen them over the other nations. However, a sage who might have written Job, Proverbs, or Ecclesiastes, who believed in the Israelite covenants, would never have mentioned the covenants in his capacity as a sage.

The Covenant Resisted

The second way to fill the silence takes the same evidence and draws the opposite conclusion — the sages hated the Israelite covenants. They had contempt for the people who forged their identity by the covenants. As an expression of their protest against the dominant ideology of Israel, they refrained from any reference to it. Therefore the corpus of literature that came from this group lacks any mention of the Israelite covenants. Again, a constructed story illustrates my point:

> Ahithophel was just leaving from a private lesson he regularly gave the prince. What crap the priests were teaching him! The prince had questioned the importance of all the history and foreign policy studies that Ahithophel required. The youth impatiently had told his instructor, "It doesn't matter whom Israel fights, as long as Yahweh is with us."
> We feed children on stories such as these, but a prince?
> The sage was unsure how to dissuade the prince from these ethereal notions, but hoped if he showed a little willful disdain that he would enable the future king to pass quickly through this pious stage.

Silent Fearing Persecution

Perhaps it was not an act of rebellion against those who represented the Israelite covenants, but rather an avoidance of conflict. In their writings the sages shunned the subject that they knew would cause them trouble. I have another story for this one:

He teaches the children of the nobles. He cannot stomach the superstitious priests who claim inside knowledge of Yahweh's preferences. He loathed the crazed prophets who stirred up the people's fears. However, he dared not allow a careless word to pass his lips, spoken against the sacred narratives. If he became careless, at the very least he might lose his job. He and his family might even be banished, or worse.

Therefore, he chose texts that avoided the ancient laws or sacred stories. Other schools used Israelite covenant texts all the time. He however would rather employ writings from his own guild, writings that studiously avoided the old pious stories. Once when a student referred to "Father Abraham," he sent her home and told her not to come back. He regarded the ancient stories as good only for the very young and the very old. But he kept his mouth shut. When accused of ignoring the sacred tales, he would defend himself saying:

"I too teach about King Solomon, who was the son and heir of the great King David."

But he doesn't say that his Solomon is the wise decider between mothers, whose covenant with Yahweh took place in Gibeah, not Sinai. In Gibeah, Yahweh appeared to Solomon and promised him wisdom as well as riches and fame (1 Kings 3).

The sage never taught the Solomon who inherited David's office, the divinely appointed throne. He never spoke of Solomon the moral failure, whose idolatry becomes a theological explanation for Israel's decline.

If the sages had known the Israelite covenants, they would have mentioned them. It is implausible to not speak of something when one disagrees strongly with it. So I suggest another way to fill the silence:

The Covenant Ignored

The fourth explanation of the silence is that the sages were ignorant of the Israelite covenants or at least had no interest in them. The controversies and positions argued by the David parties, Saul parties, parties representing the different factions of priests, the guilds, the various palace factions before the exile, the prophetic enthusiasts who threw their support to one or another group or faction, all these controversies scarcely touched the sages. For the sages, the special covenant claims of ancient Israel are sectarian disputes of little concern to them.

> Havah, the sage, had just come from the school where she had experienced a rather exhilarating debate with her former teacher on the interpretation of the ancient story of Job. Her teacher claimed that Job proved the faithfulness of Yahweh despite all appearances. But Havah argued that the story challenges the *ḥesed* of Yahweh.
>
> Afterwards, her teacher complimented her on her use of argument, but would not concede the point, not directly anyway. How good it felt to win a dispute with the old man. And in public, too.
>
> She could almost tolerate her class of palace brats, barely out of puberty, training to be lower level bureaucrats for the future king. But they would never excel in Phoenician grammar if they didn't apply themselves.

Havah had a public disputation with her teacher. Their discussion of God did not refer to the Israelite covenants. However, their conversation clearly demonstrated that they were Yahwists. In this silence, the sages were scarcely aware of the Israelite covenant theology.

Conclusion

To review, the first explanation of wisdom's silence regarding covenantal theology is that the silence is the unmentioned basis that stands behind all that the sages spoke. There would then be no distinct sapiential point of view distinguished from the other parts of the Bible. The second explanation — that the sages as a distinct group opposed the teachings and influence of another recognizable group or groups, groups that base their belief system and their sacred narrative on one or more of the Israelite covenants — suggests that the sages who wrote the Hebrew wisdom books simply avoided any reference to the hated doctrines. They remained silent as a protest, an open and defiant rejection of the covenant theologies so popular in the ancient Israelite communities. Alternately, in a third explanation, they remained silent because if they spoke their position the other groups would persecute them, marginalize them, and cut them off from access to power.

I choose the fourth option: that the sages did not regard teaching of the Israelite covenants to be important. This position best explains the data. It is plausible psychologically, and it provides a rich textured view of Israelite society, avoiding some of the more monolithic reconstructions. The portrait of ancient Israel that it presents is one where everybody does not think that the same things were important. The sages ignored the covenantal ideas in their writings because they were concerned about other things. This suggests that we change our thinking.

De-centering the Covenant

Many have insisted on interpreting all that Israel produced as reflections upon the Israelite covenants, and have regarded the absence in wisdom literature as aberrant. But Israelite society was more complex than that. There were many groups regarded as Israelite by themselves and by others, but who would not identify with any of the Israelite covenants. This takes the Israelite covenants from the center of Israelite consciousness. If one de-centers the covenant in this way, theologies will have to change. A de-centered view of the covenant would mean that:

1. Israel was less distinctive when compared to the other nations.
2. Israel was more diverse, more divided than previously imagined.
3. There was an uneasy tolerance between the groups.

There is a distinct implied authorial group created by the reading of the Hebrew wisdom books. As a shorthand, I call them sages. They were diplomats, counselors to the king, teachers to the elite young, armchair philosophers. They developed a literary tradition by collecting earlier rural traditions and adding to them. Their belief system depended upon a certain understanding of the physical universe, that it works independently and consistently, and that it contains embedded within it sufficient information to discern its meaning. (Later sages would dispute this.) They believed that a trustworthy, fair and sometimes benevolent God (Yahweh) has provided this, and secured the system.

Their implied covenant with God resembles the covenant God made with Noah:

Then God said to Noah and to his sons with him, "As for me, I am establishing my covenant with you and your descendants after you, and with every living creature that is with you, the birds, the domestic animals, and every animal of the earth with you, as many as came out of the ark. I establish my covenant with you, that never again shall all flesh be cut off by the waters of a flood, and never again shall there be a flood to destroy the earth." (Gen 9:8-11)

The flood represented chaos and unpredictability, an unstable universe liable to collapse on itself at any moment, held back only by God's benevolent hand. By promising never to do that again, God promised stability and predictability. It was this predictability that the sages assumed to validate their observations, what they observed as tendencies upon which they could base future predictions. What happens when the sage loses confidence in the predictability of nature, when God seems to have violated the Noachic covenant?

I have one final story. This one also visits Havah. Now she is old and has become skeptical about the wisdom enterprise. The sages do not have the comfort and certainty of the Israelite covenants to assure them of God's faithfulness. When wisdom fails them, they have nothing.

Havah, the sage, now an old woman, had seen her students become teachers who in turn saw their students take on this venerable occupation. She had also seen some of her charges take the reins of the Israelite government, its provinces and colonies. She had reason to feel satisfied with a life well lived.

But she had also seen disturbing tendencies within her nation, as the values and aspirations of her people were turned aside so that a privileged few could accumulate even more wealth and power. Havah felt depressed. The years seemed almost too much for her to bear.

She would put stylus to tablet one more time. The germ of her new work was not an idea, or a new reflection on an older work, but rather a single word that swirled through her consciousness like a death rattle: *hebel!* It means "emptiness," "absurdity," or "futility." She called one of her scribes into the chambers where she spent almost all of her time now, and he looked at her, waiting expectantly.

"Futility! Utter futility! All is futile! What real value is there in all the gains one makes beneath the sun? . . ." The scribe wrote furiously to keep up.

QUESTIONS FOR REVIEW

Q What are the three major covenantal themes?

Q Why do the Hebrew wisdom books not mention key Israelite themes?

Q What are the possible covenantal references in Hebrew wisdom?

Q What is meant by "de-centering" the covenant?

KEY WORDS

– Covenant, *Berît*

– Sages

– Noachic covenant

FOR FURTHER READING

Sheppard, Gerald T. *Wisdom as a Hermeneutical Construct: A Study in the Sapientializing of the Old Testament.* BZAW 151. Berlin: de Gruyter, 1980.

6. Sophia and Simon:
The Two Poles of Ben Sira's Affection

"Then the Creator of all things gave me a command,
and my Creator chose the place for my tent.
He said, 'Make your dwelling in Jacob,
and in Israel receive your inheritance.'"

SIRACH 24:8

How glorious he was, surrounded by the people,
as he came out of the house of the curtain.
Like the morning star among the clouds,
like the full moon at the festal season;
like the sun shining on the temple of the Most High,
like the rainbow gleaming in splendid clouds.

SIRACH 50:5-7

In such a diffuse book as Sirach, one looks in vain for a single organizing principle. The two figures, Sophia, the personification of Wisdom in the Hebrew tradition, and Simon II, high priest in Jerusalem and a contemporary of Ben Sira, provide a structuring grid by which we can understand at least some of Ben Sira's major concerns. Sophia and Simon appear at key moments in the book and provide a way to understand the whole. And in Ben Sira's most influential turn, he connects Sophia with Torah. No sage before him ever dreamed of doing such a thing.

Ben Sira mentions Simon in one passage only (Sir 50:1-24), towards the end of the book, the climax of the long poem, "In Praise of the Ancestors." But we are prepared to meet Simon by earlier references to priestly activities, to Aaron, the first high priest, and to the temple. Ben Sira's primary activity was teaching a school for young, elite Judeans. Perhaps he taught Simon's children. Ben Sira profoundly transformed wisdom by linking wisdom with Torah. He continued a tradition of sycophancy, where wisdom always serves the ruling class, teaching their children, turning their decrees into enforced policy. Ben Sira took it to extremes in his admiration for the high priest of Jerusalem. James Crenshaw has observed another aspect of Ben Sira's weakness:

> In his flight to areas free from empirical verification, Sirach has ceased to walk in the steps of former sages for whom experience was the ground of all knowledge. . . . In his unwillingness to subject his theory to empirical verification, Sirach approaches bad faith, for the inner dialogue between conviction and reality is silenced once and for all.[1]

The First Pole: Sophia

At almost dead center, and arguably the lynchpin that structures what is otherwise quite a diffuse book, one finds a hymn (Sir 24).[2] Lady Wisdom speaks in the first person. Ben Sira based his poem on the hymn to Wisdom in Proverbs 8, written hundreds of years earlier. She declares herself a goddess, or nearly so. Ben Sira takes these ideas and refashions them. In his version, she sings her own praises and declares herself a source of life.

By referring to Sophia (the Greek word for Wisdom), Ben Sira taps into a venerable subject found within the older wisdom writings. As George Nicklesberg notes, "The chronological starting point for his drama of salvation is not Mount Sinai or even the Exodus. In the beginning was Wisdom."[3] "Wisdom was created before all other things" (Sir 1:4). Proverbs 8 describes Hokmah as daughter of Yahweh, present at the beginning of

---

1. James L. Crenshaw, *Urgent Advice and Probing Questions: Collected Writings on Old Testament Wisdom* (Macon: Mercer University Press, 1995), 60.

2. No Hebrew for this text has been discovered.

3. George W. E. Nickelsburg, *Jewish Literature Between the Bible and the Mishnah: A Historical and Literary Introduction* (Philadelphia: Fortress, 1981), 61.

creation. The author of Proverbs celebrates Hokmah's wild power and sexual energy. He depicts her seducing the young men to follow her way and eat with her in her house.

Ben Sira takes his ideas from Proverbs without much change except that he adds a short narrative. In his story, Sophia had lived the life of an international traveler. She had "covered the earth like a mist" (Sir 24:3b), and "over every people and nation [she] held sway" (24:6b). For some reason that Ben Sira does not explain, Sophia begins to look for a home, but she does not find one: "Among all these I sought a resting place" (24:7). Then God chooses a place for her and commands her to occupy it.

> "Then the Creator of all things gave me a command, and my Creator chose the place for my tent." (24:8)

The word "command" is a strange one in this context. It might be used to express how important God sees the location of Sophia's home. Or perhaps it gives indication of Sophia's unwillingness or reluctance to follow the direction, thus the need for a command so that God ensures her compliance. In any case, it suggests that the limitation of Sophia to a single locality constitutes a radical change from what came before.

Sophia, who had traveled over all the lands and the sea, was now compelled to accept limits and boundaries, to reduce herself to one nationality alone (Jacob, another name for Israel) and only one locality: "In the holy tent I ministered before him, and so I was established in Zion" (24:10). So divine wisdom, Sophia, who had been present at the birth of the universe, now must stay in the holy tent on Mount Zion in Jerusalem. When a wise woman accepts commands and does not use her own judgment, she loses power, as if she were not wise. Sophia is such a disempowered woman. What can all this mean? What is Ben Sira trying to say? He finally reveals to his readers Wisdom's identity:

> All this [meaning all these previous references to Sophia] is the book of the covenant of the Most High God, the law[4] that Moses commanded us. (24:23)

Ben Sira proclaims that his employment of this complex tradition of Sophia is simply his way to elevate the importance of the Torah. Ben Sira

---

4. The Greek word is *nomos*, presumably from Hebrew *torah*.

says that Torah comes directly from God and precedes all the constituents of creation. By engaging in this kind of rhetoric, Ben Sira elevates the authority for what is at that very moment emerging as Israel's sacred book. Very specifically, he locates and identifies what he means by wisdom. He gives two specifications that together distinguish exactly what book he means: First, it is "the book of the covenant of the Most High God,"[5] and second, it is "the law that Moses commanded us." Did he mean the Torah, that is, the first five books of the Bible? The book of Deuteronomy? The Ten Commandments understood metaphorically as a book? He doesn't get that specific.

Wisdom, which had been international in scope, becomes in Ben Sira's hands a crude kind of patriotic enthusiasm. Ben Sira's strong nationalistic emphasis reveals itself throughout the book. In the guise of an observation, he urges his readers to avoid foreign influence. He says:

All living beings associate with their own kind, and people stick close to those like themselves. (13:16)

Although an international traveler himself, he betrays his prejudice in a prayer for Israelite victory when he says:

Put all nations in fear of you. Lift up your hands against foreign nations. (36:2-3)

He appointed a ruler for every nation, but Israel is the Lord's own portion. (17:17)

Torah, which Ben Sira never defines, becomes for him the vital thing, outweighing even wisdom in importance:

Whoever holds to the law will obtain wisdom. (15:1b)

In all wisdom there is the fulfillment of the law. (19:20)

Most revealing, Ben Sira regards more highly the ignorant person who obeys the law than a sage who ignores it. More plainly, for Ben Sira, obedience outweighs wisdom:

---

5. In Greek, *theou hypsistou,* presumably *El Elyon,* but there is no extant Hebrew text of this chapter.

> Better are the God-fearing who lack understanding than the highly in-
> telligent who transgress the law. (19:24)

"The [truly] wise will not hate the law" (33:2). He urges his readers not
to "be ashamed of the law of the Most High and his covenant" (42:2). For
the previous age, wisdom consisted in conforming to the book of nature,
the principles that God built into the universe. For Ben Sira, wisdom and
obedience to the law (now a book) are the same.

The Second Pole: Simon

The first of two poles along which we locate Ben Sira's affection is Sophia,
and he collapses her (Divine Wisdom) into the Torah. The other pole of
Ben Sira's affection is Simon II. Simon served as high priest in Jerusalem
from 219 to 196 B.C.E. He was contemporary with Ben Sira, and although
he died before Ben Sira wrote his book, the memory of the high priest remained fresh in the mind of this sage. During this period of Greek occupation, the high priest and his bureaucracy were the main Jewish sources of
power within the society. So, aside from overseeing the temple activities
and the rituals, the high priest was also a civic and political leader.

The older wisdom tradition before Ben Sira did not have much to say
about the Israelite priests and the cultic rituals that they performed and
oversaw. It did not oppose the work of the priest, but rather ignored it. The
priests were the guardians of distinctively Israelite rites and orders. The
sages, in contrast, kept watch over an international tradition, of which Israel was only a local representation. For this reason, when Ben Sira ad-
monishes his readers regarding the support of priests, he sounds anoma-
lous for a sage:

> With all your soul, fear the LORD and revere his priests. . . . Fear the
> LORD and honor the priest, and give him his portion, as you have been
> commanded. (7:29, 31)

Ben Sira's devotion to priests shows forth most dramatically in his extended poem (chs. 44-50) called "In Praise of the Ancestors." He discusses
at length Aaron, the first high priest, and his family and finally, Simon. Ben
Sira writes this poem as a kind of hall of fame for Israelite male heroes. The

author wrote over three times as much about Aaron as he wrote about Moses, a much more important personage in the Torah. Regarding Aaron, he said,

> [God] exalted Aaron, a holy man like Moses. . . .
> He clothed him in perfect splendor. . . . (45:6, 8)

Ben Sira goes on to speak at length regarding Aaron's liturgical garments. He notes that

> Before [the time of Aaron] such beautiful things did not exist.
> No outsider ever put them on, but only his [Aaron's] sons. (45:13)

After discussing Aaron and many other figures from the tradition, Ben Sira brings the poem to the climax with a description of Simon recessing from the temple. In their massively thorough and erudite Anchor Bible commentary, Alexander Di Lella and Patrick Skehan insist that the description of Simon is only an appendix to the poem and not part of the poem itself.[6] I do not agree, but I suppose they found, as I do, that the tribute to Simon is massively anticlimactic. Poor Ben Sira, so enthralled with the rich and powerful, cannot say enough about what Simon is wearing. He experiences a kind of religious ecstasy over the priestly couture![7] Note this example of Ben Sira's linguistic excesses when fawning over Simon:

> How glorious he was . . . as he came from the tent. . . .[8]
> When he put on his glorious robe
> and clothed himself in perfect splendor,
> when he went up to the holy altar,

---

6. Patrick W. Skehan and Alexander A. Di Lella, *The Wisdom of Ben Sira* (AB 39; New York: Doubleday, 1971), 550. See Skehan, *Studies in Israelite Poetry and Wisdom* (CBQMS 1; Washington: Catholic Biblical Association, 1971).

7. Ben Sira's obsession with fancy clothes even includes Sophia. He says concerning her, ". . . and her collar a glorious robe. Her yoke is a golden ornament, and her bonds a purple cord. You will wear her like a glorious robe, and put her on like a splendid crown" (6:29-31). But note these lines from Sirach: "Do not praise individuals for their good looks, or loathe anyone because of appearance alone" (11:2); "Do not boast about wearing fine clothes, and do not exalt yourself when you are honored" (11:4).

8. This translation is from Skehan and Di Lella, *The Wisdom of Ben Sira*, 546. The NRSV has "from the house of the curtain."

he made the court of the sanctuary glorious. . . .
And they bowed down in worship a second time
To receive the blessing from the Most High. (50:5, 11, 21)

Although the blessing upon the pronouncement of the sacred name of God comes from God, the instrument of blessing, according to Ben Sira, is the fancily dressed Simon. The people bow down towards him. The wording emphasizes the exalted position of Simon in relation to the people. The language of the poem makes it difficult to distinguish exactly the channel of divine grace (Simon) from its source, God. The people bow towards God, but face Simon as they do so.

To give this backwater, petty religious dictator the most prominent place in a list that includes Adam, Enoch, Abraham, Moses, David, and Jeremiah is Ben Sira's most spectacular gaffe. The absolute climax of the book points to a figure that history regards as undistinguished.

Ben Sira swoons in the presence of his social "betters," and it clouds his judgment. His profession of training the children of the elite in Jerusalem[9] brought him in close proximity to the rich without being rich himself. Ben Sira describes the task of the scribe: "He serves among the great and appears before rulers" (39:4). John Collins describes it this way:

> The typical scribe was not independently wealthy. Yet his way of life required a degree of leisure that was not available to craftsmen and artisans . . . (38:24). The scribe belonged to the retainer class, which served the needs of the governing class.[10]

But I note Ben Sira's troubled relationship with those richer than he, jealous, envious, and a bit resentful, reflected in this bit of advice:

A rich person will exploit you if you can be of use to him,
but if you are in need he will abandon you. . . .
When he needs you he will deceive you,
and will smile at you and encourage you. . . .

---

9. Note Ben Sira's two calls for "customers" for his schools: "Draw near to me, you who are uneducated,/and lodge in the house of instruction" (51:23); "Hear but a little of my instruction,/and through me you will acquire silver and gold" (51:28).

10. John J. Collins, *Jewish Wisdom in the Hellenistic Age* (OTL; Louisville: Westminster John Knox, 1997), 31.

He will embarrass you with his delicacies,
until he has drained you two or three times,
and finally he will laugh at you. (13:4-7)

Ben Sira loved the rich, was not rich himself, but gained a good measure of his self-worth from ingratiating himself to them. And in early second-century Palestine (we date his writing about 180 B.C.E.) the most powerful local person was the high priest, and Ben Sira swooned over the trappings of his authority.

This is what history knows about Ben Sira's Simon: in his official capacity as civic leader, he welcomed the Seleucid rulers from Syria after they had defeated the Ptolemaic Egyptian occupiers for control of Palestine and the region. Following the time that Ben Sira wrote, the Seleucids then proceeded to attack the Jewish way of life more profoundly than the Ptolemies ever had. So Simon ended up complicit in a profound attack on Jewish identity.[11] Ben Sira had made a category mistake, confusing the opulence of Simon's ceremony and his power, thinking it was his holiness, and even his wisdom.

Conclusion

Ben Sira's merging of Torah and Wisdom dramatically changed the wisdom project. Earlier wisdom's commitment to careful observation as a source of divine truth made the sages unique. Now Ben Sira tells us it is all in a book. As a result, Wisdom lost its international flavor, becoming much more a nationalistic concern. Roland Murphy[12] observed that Ben Sira wrote as if the books of Job and Qoheleth had never existed. The tradition of doubt and severe, honest questioning was lost, replaced with a pious acceptance of revealed truth. This was a large concession on Ben Sira's part. The wisdom tradition in Israel, by virtue of its uniqueness in the larger Israelite religious tradition, contributed greatly to the continuing development and creativity of Israel. The sages reminded the rest of the Israelites

11. Collins, *Jewish Wisdom in the Hellenistic Age*, 28. The whole passage has a Hellenistic ring to it, because of its emphasis on spectacle as the way to win glory.

12. Introduction to NRSV Sirach, *The New Oxford Annotated Bible* (New York: Oxford University Press, 1991), 86 (Apocrypha).

that other peoples, not only Israelites, had wisdom and could read the "book" of nature. They reminded the Israelites that everything, even the most closely held truths, could be questioned. By completely identifying this wisdom, previously international in nature, with "the law that Moses commanded us," Crenshaw has observed:

> How different this view of the sages' intellectual sphere was from earlier understandings where the study of nature and humane experience seemed to suffice. Nothing could be further from the old view of free inquiry than Sirach's warning against probing into things which were too difficult or defied all attempts to answer. Activity that once seemed to constitute the natural domain of sages is here called meddling into God's secrets.[13]

In spite of the attention that Ben Sira gives to Sophia, ultimately he uses her to limit the options of his students and close them off from other possibilities or dangerous questioning. Ben Sira taught classes. His students were the youth of the rich. The challenge to the students was to forge an identity in the midst of a Hellenistic world. Wisdom had traditionally been associated with internationalism and openness to foreign cultures and alien ideas. Ben Sira sums up wisdom in a book presumably untainted by dangerous, new ideas. In Ben Sira's reflection on the divine will, the Creator commands Sophia to settle down and to inhabit only one country, the nation of Israel. Ben Sira's God does not want his people to see wisdom as a possession of other lands.

The challenge to Ben Sira's community from the powerful influence of the dominating Greek culture resembles problems faced in every age and society. How can one navigate between the competing claims of religious tradition and nationalistic aspirations? The temptation to close in to one's own kind, to circle the wagons and protect from foreign pollution, remains alluring. The wisdom tradition has suggested that we look for common ground between the competing voices. Ben Sira, one of the last in a great line of Israelite intellectuals, chooses a different path.

13. James L. Crenshaw, *Old Testament Wisdom: An Introduction* (Atlanta: John Knox, 1981), 57.

QUESTIONS FOR REVIEW

Q What is Simon's relationship to Sirach?

Q What is Sophia's relationship to Torah?

Q Where does Sophia find a home? What is its significance?

Q Is Sophia a "disempowered woman"? Why or why not?

Q How did Ben Sira change the relationship of wisdom to law?

Q What is Ben Sira's attitude towards wealth?

Q How did the influence of Hellenism affect this book?

KEY WORDS

– "In Praise of the Ancestors"

– Sophia

– Simon

– Torah

– Aaron

FOR FURTHER READING

Collins, John J. *Jewish Wisdom in the Hellenistic Age*. OTL. Louisville: Westminster John Knox, 1997.

Di Lella, Alexander A. "Conservative and Progressive Theology: Sirach and Wisdom." *CBQ* 28 (1966): 129-54.

7. The Conservatism of Pseudo-Solomon

For our allotted time is the passing of a shadow,
and there is no return from our death,
because it is sealed up and no one turns back.

WISDOM OF SOLOMON 2:5

But the righteous live forever,
and their reward is with the Lord;
the Most High takes care of them.

WISDOM OF SOLOMON 5:15

The three books of Hebrew wisdom, Job, Proverbs, and Qoheleth, made a unique and positive contribution to Israelite religious literature because (a) they emphasized observation as a reliable source of religious knowledge rather than direct revelation from God;[1] (b) they remained open to questions and doubt; and (c) they listened to and incorporated the religious ideas of other cultures and ethnicities. The Wisdom of Solomon came afterwards, when the influence of Hellenism had changed forever the ways that the Israelite sages thought.

---

1. Although Job received a direct revelation from God, the author of Job disparaged God's direct revelation, elevating instead Job's wise judgment, which came from observation.

Although Pseudo-Solomon (what we call the author) wrote the book in Greek rather than Hebrew, the book is unmistakably part of the biblical wisdom corpus. The author uses wisdom vocabulary and literary images that he borrows from the earlier Hebrew texts, but he transforms the wisdom tradition to suit the new cultural context. (a) Whereas the older sages appealed to their own careful observation as a source of divine truth, Pseudo-Solomon appeals to the sacred history, particularly the stories in Genesis and Exodus. (b) Whereas the more ancient wisdom traditions explored the possibilities of sacred doubt and questioning, Pseudo-Solomon appealed to authority and tradition to shut down debate. For the first time in the wisdom tradition, doubt became a sin. (c) Whereas the ancient wisdom traditions borrowed freely from other cultures, Pseudo-Solomon regarded the surrounding Hellenistic culture as a threat. He wrote to promote Israelite exceptionalism and nationalism and to protect young people from the dangers of Greek thinking and Greek values. He does, however, move easily in the rarified atmosphere of Hellenistic philosophy and metaphysical speculation, introducing new concepts to the Israelite discussions of God, concepts he likely learned through his contact with Greek writings and Greek teachers. Pseudo-Solomon, while employing these Greek concepts, does so in the service of a conserving impulse. He tries to hold back the Hellenistic flood, which to his mind threatened to wash away Israelite religious identity.

The first section of the book (chapters 1–5 or 1–6)[2] concerns the problem of evil. The sages frequently considered the tension between the world as it should be and the world as people actually experienced it. Pseudo-Solomon recognized that in this life a righteous person may die unfairly. But he promises reward and compensation for such a righteous person in an afterlife.

Early in his career, Alexander Di Lella wrote a compelling and influential article contrasting the books of Sirach and the Wisdom of Solomon. He characterized Sirach as "conservative" and the Wisdom of Solomon as "progressive" in their response to the larger Hellenistic culture.[3] He defines

---

2. The other two sections do not impress. The second describes and celebrates Lady Wisdom, and the third consists mostly of poetic expansions and reflections from the books of Genesis and Exodus.

3. Alexander A. Di Lella, "Conservative and Progressive Theology: Sirach and Wisdom," *CBQ* 28 (1966): 129-54. Taking a somewhat different perspective, Bruce Metzger asserts that ". . . the Wisdom of Solomon . . . is concerned to unite the conventional piety of or-

"conservatives" as those who preserve the ancient way. "Progressives" are those who introduce new ideas into the tradition.

Both the Wisdom of Solomon and Ben Sira receive and pass on the ancient Israelite wisdom tradition that they received from the Hebrew books of Job, Proverbs, and Qoheleth. But these newer sages, Ben Sira and Pseudo-Solomon, came in a time when Greek culture dominated the Diaspora Jewish community. These books both respond to the profound intellectual challenge offered by the Hellenistic culture, which remained a heavy presence in the region throughout the period of their composition. Sirach came considerably earlier,[4] and probably faced a dramatically less volatile situation, not having experienced the persecution against the Jews by Antiochus IV, king of Syria (175-163 B.C.E.). However, both books show the significant Hellenistic imprint upon the lives of the Jewish communities of the eastern Mediterranean.

Di Lella defines conservatives as those who held to the essential elements of their ethnic Judaism by supporting the ancient ways. Progressives were those who explored Hellenistic ideas even at the risk of their Jewish identity. Most scholars claim that Pseudo-Solomon wrote for apostate Jews who had rejected their Jewish roots and practices in favor of Hellenistic culture and philosophy. A description in 1 Maccabees coming from a roughly similar time mentions apostate Jews who reject Jewish practice and even try to undo their circumcisions: "So they built a gymnasium in Jerusalem, according to Gentile custom, and removed the marks of circumcision, and abandoned the holy covenant. They joined with the Gentiles and sold themselves to do evil" (1 Macc 1:14-15). Pseudo-Solomon reports on a similar faction who despised the law. He describes the ungodly as saying that the righteous one "reproaches us for sins against the law" (Wis 2:12). Therefore, it is reasoned, Pseudo-Solomon's audience was those who disparaged the Jewish law.

Di Lella calls Pseudo-Solomon progressive because he introduced the

---

thodox Judaism with the Greek philosophical spirit current at that time in Alexandria"; Metzger, *An Introduction to the Apocrypha* (New York: Oxford University Press, 1957), 66. As will become clear, I am closer to Metzger, who firmly roots Pseudo-Solomon in conventional piety.

4. Along with John Collins, I prefer to stay agnostic on the dating of the Wisdom of Solomon and move on to other issues. I note especially what Collins says about the ambiguity of dating this material; *Jewish Wisdom in the Hellenistic Age* (OTL; Louisville: Westminster John Knox, 1997), 179.

idea of immortality and the afterlife as a response to the problem of evil. Pseudo-Solomon says, "For God created us for incorruption, and made us in the image of his own eternity" (Wis 2:23). This idea of life after death was only newly introduced to the Jewish community. One finds some bare hints of immortality in the books of Daniel and 2 Maccabees: "Many of those who sleep in the dust of the earth shall awake, some to everlasting life, and some to shame and everlasting contempt. Those who are wise shall shine like the brightness of the sky, and those who lead many to righteousness, like the stars forever and ever" (Dan 12:2-3); "The King of the universe will raise us up to an everlasting renewal of life. . . . One cannot but choose . . . to cherish the hope God gives of being raised again by him . . . the Creator of the World . . . will in his mercy give life and breath back to you again" (2 Macc 7:9, 14, 23).

"How is it fair that the righteous suffer?" the sages had always asked. Pseudo-Solomon assures them not to worry. After they die, the righteous will receive their reward and recompense in heaven. "Their hope is full of immortality," he asserts (3:4b). "The faithful will abide with [God] in love" (3:9b). In contrast to the Wisdom of Solomon, Di Lella observes, the book of Sirach was the more traditional of these two late wisdom books. It held faithful to ancient Israelite ideas. Ben Sira believed in an insensate Sheol, a place where the dead had no true consciousness or feelings. Pseudo-Solomon, on the other hand, embraced these new ideas regarding immortality and these new methods of reasoning that he learned from the surrounding, dominant Hellenistic culture.

Di Lella observes that the wisdom tradition had reached a stalemate in their deliberations upon the problem of evil. The sages believed in a moral universe where good was rewarded and evil punished. If one lived according to the principles of wisdom, it invariably resulted in a long and prosperous life. But the human experience of suffering and injustice told them otherwise. People who were good suffered horribly, while evil, oppressive figures lived comfortable lives of prosperity and ease. Pseudo-Solomon seeks to mediate these two positions. Di Lella states, "Only the progressive Pseudo-Solomon provides an adequate and satisfying solution to the vexing problem of retribution." Pseudo-Solomon declared that rewards and punishments are distributed *after* death. "The consoling truth of blessed immortality [is] the *ultimate* answer to the problem of retribution."[5]

---

5. Di Lella, "Conservative and Progressive Theology," 151.

All of the Hebrew wisdom writings up to this point struggled over this disconnect between human experience (which includes justice not requited) and belief in a balanced universe. Pseudo-Solomon argued that God's punishment of the wicked, though delayed, is sure to come and that those who suffer in this life will receive compensation in life after death. In the afterlife God would reward human righteousness. God had not adequately compensated the upright in the present world and would thus bring things into balance in the next life. This raw and unproven idea moves Pseudo-Solomon to new structures of thinking. He did not set out to write a treatise on immortality, but rather to address this age-old question: how can we assert the goodness of God in the presence of evil and suffering? This question (and its unsatisfactory divine answer) had silenced Job. This question had moved Qoheleth to subvert all the basic assumptions of traditional piety. Perhaps the Israelites reflected upon this question more deeply than any other culture or religion, but they ultimately came up empty. However, they had never seriously considered how something that happens after death could change their perspective.

The surrounding cultures thought about the dead all the time. The early Israelite community taught against the prevailing belief that the dead, one's ancestors, were deeply involved and invested in the lives of the living. They rejected the notion that their people should both feed and placate their departed family members. Israelite religion rarely made explicit claim regarding the fate of these ancestors, but prohibited the summoning of the dead for any purpose: "Do not turn to mediums or wizards; do not seek them out, to be defiled by them" (Lev 19:31; see also Lev 20:6, 27; Deut 18:11). (The incident with King Saul and the medium at Endor [1 Samuel 28] is the exception that proved the rule.) Mosaic law declared the realm of the dead and dead bodies (of both human and animal) unclean and defiling: "Command the Israelites to put out of the camp . . . everyone who is unclean through contact with a corpse" (Num 5:2; see also 9:6-10). See also Lev 11:31-32: "These are unclean for you . . . whoever touches one of them when they are dead shall be unclean until the evening. And anything upon which any of them falls when they are dead shall be unclean." By the first century, only the demon-possessed and predatory animals inhabited the burial sites, located outside the common living space. Therefore, the earlier Israelite sages did not consider that the fate of the dead contributed anything to the problem of evil.

Pseudo-Solomon crossed over and explored this forbidden realm, the realm of the dead. In his view of immortality, the righteous receive immortal life as a gift, while the wicked are punished with death.[6] This idea becomes part of how Christianity and Islam explain the presence of evil and the unfairness of death.[7] It is an important teaching in Judaism as well.[8]

This is why Pseudo-Solomon is a conservative rather than a progressive work: Pseudo-Solomon delivers his new idea (divine retribution in the afterlife) to shore up the old notion of divine retribution. He turns people back from what he regards as the abyss of doubt, so they could once again express confidence in divine competence and faithfulness. Instead of embracing religious ambiguity as did the ancient Hebrew sages, Pseudo-Solomon condemns doubt. He regards "putting God to the test" as an act of "distrust" (Wis 1:2). Those who doubt are guilty of "perverse" (1:3) and "foolish thoughts" (1:5). "[God] is found [he writes] by those who do not put him to the test" (1:2a).

The law of retribution argued that the universe was fair and balanced. But it consistently failed to explain day-to-day human experience. Pseudo-Solomon covered up this explanatory failure with a *deus ex machina*, which has always been a sloppy plot device, the last resort of a playwright bereft of ideas. At the very end, he says, God arrives to make everything

---

6. A problem obvious to anyone who reads the Wisdom of Solomon is a contradiction that apparently did not disturb Pseudo-Solomon, its author: If God punishes the wicked by causing them to die, why then do all die? Why must the righteous die with the wicked if it is a punishment for the unrighteous? See Michael Kolarcik, *The Ambiguity of Death in the Book of Wisdom 1–6* (AnBib 127; Rome: Pontifical Biblical Institute, 1991), 76-78. The fate of the unrighteous remains vague in the Wisdom of Solomon, similar to the ambiguity one finds in the Hebrew Bible and unlike the confident assertions in the New Testament.

7. These are some of the areas of compatibility between the Wisdom of Solomon and later traditional notions of the afterlife: (a) A righteous person will transcend death, defeat or overcome it. (b) The righteous receive a great reward in heaven. This compensates for their unfair suffering in life. (c) The unrighteous are excluded from blessed reward and experience death. However, the distinction between the first death (mortality) and the second death (eternal punishment) is not clearly made by Pseudo-Solomon. This distinction is very important in traditional Christian theology.

8. The book was also popular with Christians, but not because of its major themes. Rather, they liked it because of certain isolated verses that suggested to them a christological interpretation. For instance, see the discussion of Sophia as *Logos*, the persecuted righteous one, the mention of the blessed wood that brings righteousness (concerning Noah's ark), and the mention of God's divine word coming down to judge the earth (referring to the death of the firstborn in Egypt). For the early Christians, these all represent Christ. See Metzger, *An Introduction to the Apocrypha*, 75-76.

turn out well. The Jewish teaching regarding the justice of God had nearly failed because of the sufferings of the exilic community of Israel. Pseudo-Solomon's narrative breathed new life into this timeworn doctrine. Because later Jews and especially Christians accepted most of Pseudo-Solomon's narrative in their teachings, the influence of retributive theology remains the dominant narrative used and continues to prevail over most other attempts to explain the evil and unfairness of life.[9] Pseudo-Solomon conserves an ancient tradition.

Di Lella argues that Pseudo-Solomon, coming upon an intractable theological problem, "thought outside the box" and thus developed an innovative way to solve the dilemma. How can one reconcile the goodness of God with the presence of innocent suffering while the guilty escape unscathed? By asserting that God metes out his justice in the afterlife, Pseudo-Solomon changed the way his community understood suffering. For Di Lella, this makes him a progressive.

On the contrary, the distinct character of Pseudo-Solomon's contribution comes clear when we compare the Wisdom of Solomon to two of his wisdom forebears, the books of Job (briefly) and Qoheleth (at length). If we define (again using Di Lella's terms) conservatives as those who seek to preserve older ways and to prevent change, how might we categorize the Wisdom of Solomon when compared to these books? Job questions God's justice, while Pseudo-Solomon finds new reasons to accept it.[10] Job's reckless declaration of his own innocence at Yahweh's expense shatters the ancient traditional affirmations about the goodness and reliability of God. Pseudo-Solomon supports these affirmations at every juncture. Job raises questions while Pseudo-Solomon suppresses them. The book of Job represents a more progressive approach to the questions of innocent suffering than the Wisdom of Solomon. The Wisdom of Solomon uses a new idea (reward and punishment in the afterlife) to shore up a very old and oppressive idea, the law of retribution.

The Wisdom of Solomon is more closely connected with Ecclesiastes than the book of Job. Pseudo-Solomon closely reproduces teachings of the Hebrew sage known as Qoheleth. While not quoting, some of his writing

9. The essence of retributive theology is not that the retribution occurs *in this life.* Rather, that is incidental to its teaching. The real teaching is that all iniquity is punished by God, inevitably.

10. See my *The Betrayal of God: Ideological Conflict in Job* (Louisville: Westminster John Knox, 1990), particularly chs. 3 and 4.

resembles the world-weary attitude of the author of the much older book. Pseudo-Solomon tells a story of wicked men in their conflict with a solitary righteous man.[11] The scene opens when these wicked men discuss among themselves life's meaning. "Short and sorrowful is our life," one laments, "and there is no remedy when a life comes to its end" (Wis 2:1). How should they conduct themselves in the light of this hopeless pronouncement? One of them advises that if this is all life offers, they must take pleasure in it to the fullest. "Come, therefore, let us enjoy the good things that exist," he says (2:6).

The position of the ungodly strongly resembles some of the arguments found in the book of Ecclesiastes. These are quotations from the Wisdom of Solomon: "For our allotted time is the passing of a shadow, and there is no return from our death, because it is sealed up and no one turns back" (Wis 2:5) "Come, therefore, let us enjoy the good things that exist, and make use of the creation to the full as in youth" (2:6). Note similar sentiment found in "Enjoy Life, Qoheleth": "There is nothing better for mortals than to eat and drink, and find enjoyment in their toil" (Eccl 2:24; also 8:15). "For there is no enduring remembrance of the wise or of fools, seeing that in the days to come all will have been long forgotten" (2:16; see also 3:20; 9:10).

This conversation among the ungodly takes a sinister turn when one of them suggests that, because God does not see and cannot punish them, they should feel free to attack the weak and powerless. "Let us oppress the righteous poor man; let us not spare the widow or regard the gray hairs of the aged" (Wis 2:10). At this point, the righteous man enters the narrative. This person had criticized the behavior and belief system of the wicked men, and they hate him for it. "He reproaches us for sins against the law, and accuses us of sins against our training" (2:12). He has bragged to them of his trust in God and his confidence that God will always defend him. "He calls the last end of the righteous happy, and boasts that God is his father" (2:16). The ungodly feel guilty because of the constant presence and pressure of this righteous man. "The very sight of him is a burden to us," they say (2:15). Therefore, they decide to make him an example to disprove

---

11. I have used the words "ungodly" and "wicked" to describe this group. The author scarcely identifies them in 1:16: "But *the ungodly* by their words and deeds summoned death; considering him a friend, they pined away and made a covenant with him, because they are fit to belong to his company."

his false claims. "Let us test him with insult and torture, so that we may find out how gentle he is . . . for, according to what he says, he will be protected" (2:19-20). Thus they prove (as they believe) that their philosophy of life is superior to his. Even though he was righteous, God did not protect him. They tortured and killed him, but there was no divine intervention. However, the narrator observes, "Thus they reasoned, but they were led astray, for their wickedness blinded them, and they did not know the secret purposes of God, nor hoped for the wages of holiness" (2:21-22).

It is not Pseudo-Solomon who speaks these skeptical words in chapter 2, but rather, a character in a story that Pseudo-Solomon made up, dialogue in a narrative. Pseudo-Solomon disapproves of these characters and what they say. Pseudo-Solomon asserts that the people who question the meaningfulness of life (as do some in the earlier wisdom tradition) act with oppressive violence. Therefore, Pseudo-Solomon, in this context, regarded people like Qoheleth the skeptic (writing hundreds of years earlier) as purveyors of dangerous, sinful ideas, ideas that he, Pseudo-Solomon, links with violence and implicates in oppression. For Pseudo-Solomon, the voice that questions divine faithfulness, saying, "For we were born by mere chance" (2:2a), is dripping with evil intent: "Let us lie in wait for the righteous man, because he is inconvenient to us and opposes our actions" (2:12).

Pseudo-Solomon responds to Qoheleth's skepticism, or perhaps a skeptical "school" within his own community of the sages. He faults them, because neither the ungodly in Pseudo-Solomon's narrative nor Qoheleth had taken into account what an afterlife would mean for their moral and intellectual choices. By impugning the motives of those who raise questions (because they use their philosophizing as an excuse for evil behavior), Pseudo-Solomon believes he can pull his students back from the abyss of their own questions.

This story, which covers part of chapter 1 and all of chapter 2, does not continue until chapter 5, and there things have changed considerably. Pseudo-Solomon describes the scene: "Then the righteous will stand with great confidence in the presence of those who have oppressed them and those who make light of their labors" (5:1).[12]

This company of the righteous has passed through death to some

12. The NRSV translation reflects the sense that the singular word ("the righteous one") might have become here a collective noun, "the righteous ones."

manner of existence on the other side. Do the ungodly see their victim back from the dead in some horrific vision or because they too are dead, assembled in some final judgment? Pseudo-Solomon does not explain. John Collins describes this as "an apocalyptic scene."[13] In any case, the ungodly see that the righteous have received their reward. They have become "numbered among the children of God,[14] their lot among the holy ones" (5:5). They have become members of the divine council, joined to the company of angels.[15] These wicked ones had not considered that their victim would get such a reward *after* they had killed him.

Finally, Pseudo-Solomon declares that these wicked individuals, who so obsessed over the brutal reality of human death, would die indeed, would experience the death they expected. George Nickelsburg observes:

> In all these things they [the ungodly] were wrong, but in one way they were right. They face the extinction they anticipated. This is so because they themselves summoned death (1:16), and now it claims them. Their nihilistic belief led to sinful actions, and these are punished by the annihilation they had posited in the first place. On the other hand the righteous will live forever (5:15-16). Theirs is the gift of immortality in which they had believed.[16]

These wicked men would "become dishonored corpses, and an outrage among the dead forever" (4:18).

There are the various theories as to what Pseudo-Solomon actually meant with regard to death and immortality in this passage. The two most common are:

1. The death of the wicked refers to eternal death, not the death which all experience. Immortality (forever-lasting life after physical death) is a reward God gives to the righteous. This interpretation agrees with the standard rabbinic and first-century Christian notions of the afterlife.

13. Collins, *Jewish Wisdom in the Hellenistic Age,* 179.

14. Both these terms, "the sons of God" and "the holy ones" (NRSV "saints"), commonly refer to angels. See my discussion in *Twilight of the Gods: Polytheism in the Hebrew Bible* (Louisville: Westminster John Knox, 2005), chs. 3 and 4.

15. See my *Twilight of the Gods,* chs. 3 and 4.

16. George W. E. Nickelsburg, *Jewish Literature Between the Bible and the Mishnah: A Historical and Literary Introduction* (Philadelphia: Fortress, 1981), 177-78.

2. Death for the wicked constitutes nonexistence or a shadowy existence in the netherworld of Sheol. Whereas the older Hebrew writing consigned all people to this shadowy existence, Pseudo-Solomon sends the unrighteous there as a punishment. The righteous enjoy eternal heavenly life.

These two great, muscular efforts by later traditions sought to compel Pseudo-Solomon to agree with either one external standard (first-century Jewish and Christian orthodoxy) or another (ancient Israelite beliefs regarding Sheol). I suggest a third explanation for this sage's muddle.

Interpreters cannot succeed in conforming Pseudo-Solomon to either the way Israelites believed in earlier periods or the way later Christians and Jews believed. The text remains ambiguous and ill fits these other thought-systems. On this issue, Pseudo-Solomon is confused. On the one hand, he embraces the popular Hellenistic thinking regarding the immortality and preexistence of the soul. On the other hand, he is a child of the Hebrew Bible. Its terms and concepts shaped and structured his thinking. Therefore, his ideas hang together poorly. Either he has not realized that the ancient Israelite agnosticism regarding Sheol differs from Greek notions of the immortal soul or he realizes it, does not know what to do with it, and dumps the problem in the reader's lap.

Earlier sages urged their readers and students to attend to and to trust the validity of their human experience over against theological affirmations concerning the nature of God. Pseudo-Solomon tells his readers (contrary to this earlier wisdom tradition) not to believe their own experience of life. He tells them instead to trust him, the last of the sages. He assures them that the wicked have long, miserable, unproductive lives while the godly will gain immortality in the next world. Both of these assertions are unprovable and only available by means of revelation or many layers of inference. One cannot confirm the existence of an afterlife through human perception or experience. Whatever may or may not happen in the afterlife, it is not available to human perceptual knowledge or human memory. It becomes a matter of faith and optimism.

When the sages experienced suffering, they questioned the justice of God. They attempted to resolve this dilemma in different ways. Different ones within the sapiential community would claim one or more of the following:

1. All suffering is deserved. People suffer as a result of sin.
2. Suffering purifies and cleanses a person's soul.
3. Suffering is instructive.
4. There is no adequate answer to the problem of suffering.
5. God is unjust.[17]

The sages never came to consensus, but within their discourse they accomplished the following things: By their emphasis on experience and judgment (because they did not appeal to special revelation or religious authority) they gave worth and dignity to the independence of the human spirit. Each individual's perspective or voice must not be ignored, but must remain as an angle of vision that stands against the most authoritative religious pronouncements. Pseudo-Solomon offers a different approach when he claims that the magnitude of the innocent suffering pales against the prospect of their future reward.

The earlier Hebrew sages taught the Israelites to deal with and find benefit in theological ambiguity. They asserted that binary answers (yes or no, good or bad, in-group or out-group) seldom sufficed for real-world difficulties. By their rhetoric and their teaching they allowed that truth often lies at the collision of two or more contradictory ideas. The Hebrew sages nurtured and kept alive the ancient Israelite tradition of sacred doubt.

The "school" that produced the books of Job and Ecclesiastes was characterized by their openness to ideas from beyond the Israelite society, their willingness to entertain seditious thoughts about their traditions, their ruthless honesty in self-examination, their willingness to confront the powerful, the high level of their literary accomplishments, and their embrace of ambiguity. Pseudo-Solomon changed key elements of that tradition in the service of his own theological project. He sought to protect God from accusation of unfairness and claimed that the law of retribution still worked, in spite of evidence of human experience. He introduces a whole new source of knowledge, but one which was unavailable to observation. Humans must trust in a future eschatological rectification in heaven for all the injustice on earth. One may work for justice in this life, but ultimately it will only come from God, after death.

17. See James L. Crenshaw's introduction to *Theodicy in the Old Testament* (IRT 4; Philadelphia: Fortress and London: SPCK, 1983).

The Wisdom of Solomon is conservative in its stance, perspective, and outlook. He supports the ancient piety which claimed that the righteous are always rewarded and the wicked punished. Rich people use this belief to justify their accumulation of wealth and to excuse themselves from responsibility for the sufferings of the poor. God enforces justice in the universe. If one is evil, one suffers at some point. If one is righteous, at some point one will receive a reward. Pseudo-Solomon asserts that this holds true. He argues its reliability as a fundamental principle of life. Pseudo-Solomon assures his readers that God will ultimately rectify all wrongs. The powerless, therefore, must wait passively until their redemption arrives. This "pie-in-the-sky," patient waiting discourages people from complaining about their conditions or trying to change them.

Further, Pseudo-Solomon hates the ethnic other. In his poem praising divine mercy, he describes God's near limitless patience. He gives the wicked Canaanites a lot of time to reform their ways: "But even these you spared, since they were but mortals" (12:8); "you gave them an opportunity to repent" (12:10). But Pseudo-Solomon confides to the reader the impossibility that the Canaanites would ever submit to God.[18] He says, "their origin was evil and their wickedness inborn, and . . . their way of thinking would never change. For they were an accursed race from the beginning" (12:10-11). Pseudo-Solomon maintained this fanatically anti-Canaanite stance. The language of Canaanite hatred served well to mask his hostility towards Greek domination. His attitude reflects an extreme nationalism and a deep hatred and distrust of the foreigner. He has transformed the earlier wisdom tradition of universalism, for he seeks to establish the superiority of the Jewish religion.

Thus, Pseudo-Solomon moves the wisdom tradition away from that which made it so dangerous and transgressive, its elevation of the human voice over the divine voice.

We end this book in a sad place. If you have read this book carefully, it is no secret that I prefer the wisdom of the books of Job and Ecclesiastes over the defenders of traditional piety (old and new) in the other books. The Greek

18. The Canaanites might have represented the Greeks to Pseudo-Solomon, as the ancient (for him) Egyptians represented the contemporary Egyptians, two different groups of Gentiles symbolized very differently in Pseudo-Solomon's writing. Collins, *Jewish Wisdom in the Hellenistic Age*, 218.

sages, facing a terrible threat to their identity and existence (at least they believed it was a threat), stepped back from some of the most fantastic innovations of the Hebrew sages — their openness to questioning and ambiguity, their willingness to face painful truths. However, these Greek sages carried forth the tradition and transmitted the earlier books to new audiences. The dangerous (but oh-so-necessary) teachings of Job and Ecclesiastes remain for a challenge and reminder to question authority, accept ambiguity (answers are not yes or no, black or white), not to believe everything that one is told, and to dig and dig to get to the truth — and finally, never, never blame a suffering person for his or her pain.

QUESTIONS FOR REVIEW

Q Did Solomon write this book? How do you know?

Q What are the three sections of the Wisdom of Solomon?

Q Is Pseudo-Solomon progressive or conservative? How do you know?

Q How does this book answer the problem of evil?

Q What was the traditional Hebrew attitude towards the realm of the dead?

Q What is the relationship between the Wisdom of Solomon and the book of Ecclesiastes?

Q What happens to the righteous dead according to Pseudo-Solomon? What happens to the wicked after death?

KEY WORDS

− Pseudo-Solomon

− Incorruption

− Immortality

FOR FURTHER READING

Di Lella, Alexander A. "Conservative and Progressive Theology: Sirach and Wisdom." *CBQ* 28 (1966): 129-54.

Hengel, Martin. *Judaism and Hellenism: Studies in Their Encounter in Palestine during the Early Hellenistic Period*. Trans. John Bowden. 2 vols. Philadelphia: Fortress, 1974. German ed. 1966; rev. ed. 1973.

Kolarcik, Michael. *The Ambiguity of Death in the Book of Wisdom 1–6*. AnBib 127. Rome: Pontifical Biblical Institute, 1991.

Metzger, Bruce M. *An Introduction to the Apocrypha*. New York: Oxford University Press, 1957.

Conclusion

When I consider biblical wisdom books as a whole, two narratives emerge. I cannot decide between them. The first one is a tragedy and the second a triumph.

This is the tragedy: In the midst of the rigid, patriarchal, conservative Israelite society, there emerged a more progressive movement, the wisdom tradition, the tradition of the sages. Whereas religious elite controlled most segments of Israelite society, the sages, the wisdom movement, promoted independence of thought and honest debate. The priests claimed authority from tradition and sacred texts, and the prophets received messages from God. The sages, however, trusted their own experience and observation as a source of knowledge. They fashioned a unique voice and tradition when compared to the other collections of the Hebrew Bible. Then, Greek/Hellenistic culture imposed its ideas upon the Jewish communities. This so traumatized the next generation of sages that they "sold their birthright." They surrendered central principles of the wisdom tradition. To do otherwise, they believed, would result in their extinction. So the sages made peace with the priests and conceded that Woman wisdom, their patron, was in fact the same as the Torah, the guide to behavior and belief assembled from ancient writings by the priests in the fourth century B.C.E. These third-generation sages opened the doors and allowed the diverse biblical traditions to enter in and reshape their work. Job, Proverbs, and Ecclesiastes, coming before, had not mentioned the foundational Israelite traditions of the exodus and King David nor the traditions of sacrifice and prayer characteristic of the Israelite communities. They had maintained their contribution as distinct from the other Israelite, Judean, and

111

Jewish leaders. However, Ben Sira and the Wisdom of Solomon, written after this transition, refer to the other biblical traditions without reservation.

In this tragic narrative, the sages gave up something valuable, that which made them unique. They had been an independent voice that responded in novel ways to the Israelite God Yahweh. They provided a different picture, a counterpoint to the descriptions of Yahweh in other parts of the Bible. Further, this had enabled them to criticize the prevailing Israelite religious assumptions regarding the goodness and reliability of their God. The Greek sages surrendered this independent voice when they embraced the more nationalistic and fundamentalist notions of religion, the outlook that characterized Jewish leadership in the Hellenistic period.

So in this tragic narrative, wisdom was a flash of light and fearless intellectual discourse that subsequently flamed out, subsumed by the larger though more narrowly focused Hellenistic Jewish sensibilities. However, I am suspicious of such a pat narrative, one that has painted a picture consisting of two-dimensional heroes and villains. Is there some essential wisdom "essence" possessed by the early sages, subsequently lost by the Greek Jewish sages? Suppose instead there is not a special wisdom essence to be either defended or lost. Rather, wisdom is a living tradition that responds and changes when faced with a different context.

From this perspective, the second narrative emerges, the story of wisdom's triumph. Wisdom specializes in confronting the foundational questions, but the context in which they raise these questions changes. For instance, early wisdom, the first wave, tended towards optimism and confidence. They were certain that God governed the universe with consistency and justice. But subsequent sages, confronted with tragedies, both national and personal, had this confidence shaken. These sages, the second wave, responded by questioning and challenging the basis for that earlier confidence. They considered the implications of a universe where one cannot depend upon God.

The advent of Hellenism offered a different challenge to the Jewish community and to the sages who were a part of it. This constituted a third wave. Faced with existential challenge from Hellenism, the sages responded by joining in permanent alliance with the other religious authorities in Judea and in Jewish communities throughout the eastern Mediterranean.

At the same time, they were able to achieve something in this era that no other Israelite groups could have accomplished. As in earlier ages, the Hellenistic sages remained open to new and foreign ideas. Once again, the sages sought to master useful notions from other cultures, as in previous generations they had borrowed from Egypt, Babylon, and other foreign wisdom traditions. At this time, they familiarized themselves with the occupying culture of the Greeks. While outwardly holding the line in favor of Jewish culture and Jewish identity, they also took the new ideas and worked with them to refashion their religious identity in a way that would survive the changes taking place in their world. Survive they did, and their ideas survived as well.

These are the two narratives regarding the wisdom tradition, one a tragedy and the other a triumph. Which to choose? Must one choose? We are left with an ambiguity, and this ambiguity is characteristic of the wisdom enterprise throughout. This ambiguity might be the true "essence" of the wisdom tradition. The sages modeled the ability to cope with and even thrive in conditions where firm answers remain unavailable. That is their greatest contribution.

Bibliography

Albright, William F. *From the Stone Age to Christianity: Monotheism and the Historical Process.* 2nd ed. Garden City: Doubleday, 1957.

Anderson, William H. U. *Qoheleth and Its Pessimistic Theology: Hermeneutical Struggles in Wisdom Literature.* Mellen Biblical Press Series 54. Lewiston: Mellen Biblical, 1997.

———. "Philosophical Considerations in a Genre Analysis of Qoheleth." *VT* 48 (1998): 289-300.

———. "The Poetic Inclusio of Qoheleth in Relation to 1,2 and 12,8." *SJOT* 12 (1998): 203-13.

———. "Ironic Correlations and Scepticism in the Joy Statements of Qoheleth." *SJOT* 14 (2000): 67-100.

Bailey, Kenneth E. "Women in Ben Sirach and in the New Testament." In *For Me to Live: Essays in Honor of James Leon Kelso,* ed. Robert A. Coughenour. Cleveland: Dillon/Lidederback, 1972, 56-73.

Berger, Benjamin Lyle. "Qohelet and the Exigencies of the Absurd." *BibInt* 9 (2001): 141-79.

Beuken, W. A. M., ed. *The Book of Job.* BETL 114. Leuven: Leuven University Press, 1994.

Blank, Sheldon H. "Ecclesiastes." In *IDB,* 2:7-13.

———. "Proverbs, Book of." In *IDB,* 3: 936-40.

Bostrom, Lennart. *The God of the Sages: The Portrayal of God in the Book of Proverbs.* ConBOT 29. Stockholm: Almqvist & Wiksell, 1990.

Box, G. H., and W. O. E. Oesterley. "Sirach." In *APOT* 1:268-517.

Breton, Santiago. "Qoheleth Studies." *BTB* 3 (1973): 22-50.

Brown, William P. *Ecclesiastes*. Interpretation. Louisville: Westminster John Knox, 2011.

Burkill, T. A. "Ecclesiasticus." In *IDB*, 2:13-21.

Camp, Claudia. "Woman Wisdom as Root Metaphor: A Theological Consideration." In Hoglund et al., *The Listening Heart*, 45-76.

Castellino, Giorgio. "Qohelet and His Wisdom." *CBQ* 30 (1968): 15-28.

Christianson, Eric S. *A Time To Tell: Narrative Strategies in Ecclesiastes*. JSOTSup 280. Sheffield: Sheffield Academic, 1998.

———. *Ecclesiastes through the Centuries*. Blackwell Bible Commentaries. Oxford: Blackwell, 2007.

Clarke, Ernest G. *The Wisdom of Solomon*. CBC. Cambridge: Cambridge University Press, 1973.

Clemens, David M. Review of *Symbol and Rhetoric in Ecclesiastes: The Place of Hebel in Qohelet's Work* by Douglas B. Miller. *JNES* 66 (2007): 217-21.

Clifford, Richard J. *Proverbs*. OTL. Louisville: Westminster John Knox, 1999.

Clines, David J. A. "Why Is There a Book of Job and What Does It Do to You If You Read It?" In Beuken, *The Book of Job*, 1-20.

Collins, John J. *Jewish Wisdom in the Hellenistic Age*. OTL. Louisville: Westminster John Knox, 1997.

Crenshaw, James L. "The Influence of the Wise upon Amos: The 'Doxologies of Amos' and Job 5,9-16; 9,5-10." *ZAW* 79 (1967): 42-52.

———. "Method in Determining Wisdom Influence upon 'Historical' Literature." *JBL* 88 (1969): 129-42.

———. "The Problem of Theodicy in Sirach: On Human Bondage." *JBL* 94 (1975): 47-64.

———. "The Birth of Skepticism in Ancient Israel." In *The Divine Helmsman: Studies in God's Control of Human Events, presented to Lou H. Silverman,* ed. Crenshaw and Samuel Sandmel. New York: KTAV, 1980, 1-9.

———. *Old Testament Wisdom: An Introduction*. Atlanta: John Knox, 1981. 3rd ed. Louisville: Westminster John Knox, 2010.

———. "Introduction: The Shift From Theodicy to Anthropodicy." In *Theodicy in the Old Testament*, 1-25.

———. "Qoheleth in Current Research." *HAR* 7 (1983): 41-56.

———. *A Whirlpool of Torment: Israelite Traditions of God as an Oppressive Presence*. OBT 12. Philadelphia: Fortress, 1984.

———. "The High Cost of Preserving God's Honor." *The World and I* (1987), 375-82.

———. *Ecclesiastes*. OTL. Philadelphia: Westminster, 1987.

—————. "Murphy's Axiom: Every Gnomic Saying Needs a Balancing Corrective." In Hogland et al., *The Listening Heart*, 1-17.

—————. "Ecclesiastes, Book of." In *ABD*, 2 (1992): 271-80.

—————. "Proverbs, Book of." In *ABD*, 5:513-20.

—————. "The Concept of God in Old Testament Wisdom." In Perdue, Scott, and Wiseman, *In Search of Wisdom*, 1-18.

—————. "The Eternal Gospel (Ecclesiastes 3:11)." In *Urgent Advice and Probing Questions*, 548-72.

—————. "The Perils of Specializing in Wisdom: What I Have Learned from Thirty Years of Teaching." In *Urgent Advice and Probing Questions*, 586-96.

—————. "The Shadow of Death in Qoheleth." In *Urgent Advice and Probing Questions*, 573-85.

—————. Review of *A Time to Tear Down and a Time to Build Up: A Rereading of Ecclesiastes*. *JAOS* 121 (2001): 288-89.

—————. "Qoheleth in Historical Context." *Bib* 88 (2007): 285-99.

Crenshaw, James L., ed. *Studies in Ancient Israelite Wisdom*. Library of Biblical Studies. New York: Ktav, 1976.

—————, ed. *Theodicy in the Old Testament*. IRT 4. Philadelphia: Fortress and London: SPCK, 1983.

—————, ed. *Urgent Advice and Probing Questions: Collected Writings on Old Testament Wisdom*. Macon: Mercer University Press, 1995.

Cronback, Abraham. "The Social Ideals of the Apocrypha and Pseudepigrapha." *HUCA* 18 (1943-44): 119-56.

Crüsemann, Frank. "The Unchangeable Work: The 'Crisis of Wisdom' in Koheleth." In *God of the Lowly*, ed. Willy Schottroff and Wolfgang Stegemann. Maryknoll: Orbis, 1984, 57-77.

Dahood, Mitchell. "Proverbs 8,22-31: Translation and Commentary." *CBQ* 30 (1968): 512-21.

Danker, Frederick W. "The Pessimism of Ecclesiastes." *CTM* 22 (1951): 9-32.

Davidson, A. B. "Sirach's Judgment of Women." *ExpTim* 6 (1894-95): 402-4.

Di Lella, Alexander A. "Conservative and Progressive Theology: Sirach and Wisdom." *CBQ* 28 (1966): 129-54.

Eichrodt, Walther. *Theology of the Old Testament*. Trans. John A. Baker. 2 vols. OTL. Philadelphia: Westminster, 1961-67.

Fisch, Harold. *Poetry with a Purpose: Biblical Poetics and Interpretation*. Bloomington: Indiana University Press, 1988.

Fontaine, Carol R. "Wisdom in Proverbs." In Perdue, Scott, and Wiseman, *In Search of Wisdom*, 99-114.

Forman, Charles C. "The Pessimism of Ecclesiastes." *JSS* 3 (1958): 336-43.

Fox, Michael V. "The Meaning of *Hebel* for Qohelet." *JBL* 105 (1986): 409-27.

———. "Qohelet's Epistemology." *HUCA* 58 (1987): 137-55.

———. *Qohelet and His Contradictions.* JSOTSup 71. Decatur: Almond, 1989.

———. Review of *Die Weisheit Israels — ein Fremdkörper im Alten Testament? Eine Untersuchung zum Buch der Sprüche auf dem hintergrund der ägyptischen Weisheitslehren* by Franz-Josef Steiert. CBQ 111 (1992): 134-37.

———. "The Social Location of the Book of Proverbs." In *Texts, Temples, and Traditions: A Tribute to Menahem Haran,* ed. Fox et al. Winona Lake: Eisenbrauns, 1996, 227-39.

———. "The Inner Structure of Qohelet's Thought." In *Qohelet in the Context of Wisdom,* ed. Antoon Schoors. BETL 136. Leuven: Leuven University Press and Peeters, 1998, 225-38.

———. *A Time to Tear Down and a Time to Build Up: A Rereading of Ecclesiastes.* Grand Rapids: Eerdmans, 1999.

———. *Proverbs 1-9.* AB 18A. New York: Doubleday, 2000.

———. *Ecclesiastes: The Traditional Hebrew Text with the New JPS Translation.* JPS Bible Commentary. Philadelphia: Jewish Publication Society, 2006.

———. *Proverbs 10–31.* AYB 18B. New Haven: Yale University Press, 2009.

Fritsch, Charles T. "Proverbs." In *IB,* 4 (1955): 767-957.

Gammie, John G., et al., eds. *Israelite Wisdom: Theological and Literary Essays in Honor of Samuel Terrien.* Missoula: Scholars, 1978.

Gaspar, Joseph W. *Social Ideas in the Wisdom Literature of the Old Testament.* Catholic University of America Studies in Sacred Theology, 2nd ser. 8. Washington: Catholic University of America, 1947.

Geyer, John. *The Wisdom of Solomon: Introduction and Commentary.* TBC. London: SCM, 1963.

Good, Edwin M. *Irony in the Old Testament.* Philadelphia: Westminster, 1965. Repr. Sheffield: Almond, 1981.

———. *In Turns of Tempest: A Reading of Job.* Stanford: Stanford University Press, 1990.

Gordis, Robert. *Koheleth — The Man and His World: A Study of Ecclesiastes.* 3rd ed. New York: Schocken, 1968.

Grant, Jamie A. "Wisdom and Covenant: Revisiting Zimmerli." *European Journal of Theology* 12 (2003): 103-13.

Grintz, Jehoshua M. "The Proverbs of Solomon." In Snell, *Twice-Told Proverbs and the Composition of the Book of Proverbs,* 87-114.

Habel, Norman C. *The Book of Job.* OTL. Philadelphia: Westminster, 1985.

Harrington, Daniel J. *Invitation to the Apocrypha*. Grand Rapids: Eerdmans, 1999.

Hengel, Martin. *Judaism and Hellenism: Studies in Their Encounter in Palestine during the Early Hellenistic Period*. Trans. John Bowden. 2 vols. Philadelphia: Fortress, 1974. German ed. 1966; rev. ed. 1973.

Hogland, Kenneth G., et al., eds. *The Listening Heart: Essays in Wisdom and the Psalms in Honor of Roland E. Murphy, O.Carm*. JSOTSup 58. Sheffield: JSOT, 1987.

Horne, Milton P. *Proverbs, Ecclesiastes*. Smyth & Helwys Bible Commentary. Macon: Smyth & Helwys, 2003.

Horton, Ernest Horace. "Koheleth's Concept of Opposites as Compared to Samples of Greek Philosophy and Near and Far Eastern Wisdom Classics." *Numen* 19 (1972): 1-21.

Koch, Klaus. "Is There a Doctrine of Retribution in the Old Testament?" In Crenshaw, *Theodicy in the Old Testament*, 57-87.

Kolarcik, Michael. *The Ambiguity of Death in the Book of Wisdom 1–6*. AnBib 127. Rome: Pontifical Biblical Institute, 1991.

Kovacs, Brian W. "Is There a Class-Ethic in Proverbs?" In *Essays in Old Testament Ethics: J. Philip Hyatt, in Memoriam*, ed. James L. Crenshaw and John T. Willis. New York: Ktav, 1974, 171-89.

Krüger, Thomas *Qoheleth*. Trans. O. C. Dean; ed. Klaus Baltzer. Hermeneia. Minneapolis: Fortress, 2004.

Landes, George. "Creation Tradition in Proverbs 8,22-31 and Gen 1." In *A Light unto My Path: Old Testament Studies in Honor of Jacob M. Myers*, ed. Howard N. Bream, Ralph D. Heim, and Carey A. Moore. Philadelphia: Temple University Press, 1974, 279-93.

Lang, Bernhard. *Wisdom and the Book of Proverbs: A Hebrew Goddess Redefined*. New York: Pilgrim, 1986.

———. "Wisdom." In *Dictionary of Deities and Demons in the Bible*, ed. Karel van der Toorn, Bob Becking, and Pieter W. Van der Horst. 2nd ed. Leiden: Brill and Grand Rapids: Eerdmans, 1999, 900-905.

Loader, J. A. *Polar Structures in the Book of Qohelet*. BZAW 152. Berlin: de Gruyter, 1979.

Lohfink, Norbert. "Qoheleth 5:17-19 — Revelation by Joy." *CBQ* 52 (1990): 625-35.

———. *Qoheleth*. CC. Minneapolis: Fortress, 2003.

MacDonald, Duncan Black. *The Hebrew Literary Genius: An Interpretation Be-*

ing an Introduction to the Reading of the Old Testament. Princeton: Princeton University Press, 1933. Repr. New York: Russell & Russell, 1968.

―――. *The Hebrew Philosophical Genius: A Vindication.* Princeton: Princeton University Press, 1936. Repr. New York: Russell & Russell, 1965.

Machinist, Peter. "Fate, *Miqreh* and Reason: Some Reflections on Qohelet and Biblical Thought." In *Solving Riddles and Untying Knots: Biblical, Epigraphic, and Semitic Studies in Honor of Jonas C. Greenfield,* ed. Ziony Zevit, Seymour Gitin, and Michael Sokoloff. Winona Lake: Eisenbrauns, 1995, 159-75.

McKane, William. *Prophets and Wise Men.* SBT, 2nd ser. 44. Naperville: Allenson, 1965.

McKeating, Henry. "Jesus ben Sira's Attitude to Women." *ExpTim* 85 (1973-74): 85-87.

McKenzie, John L. "Reflections on Wisdom," *JBL* 86 (1967): 1-9.

MacKenzie, R. A. F. "Ben Sira as Historian." In *Trinification of the World: A Festschrift in Honour of Frederick E. Crowe in Celebration of His 60th Birthday,* ed. Thomas A. Dunne and Jean-Marc Laporte. Toronto: Regis College Press, 1978, 313-27.

―――. *Sirach.* Old Testament Message 19. Wilmington: Glazier, 1983.

Martin, James D. "Ben Sira — A Child of His Time." In *A Word in Season: Essays in Honour of William McKane,* ed. Martin and Philip R. Davies. JSOTSup 42. Sheffield: JSOT, 1986, 141-61.

Merkin, Daphne. "Ecclesiastes: A Depressive's Lament." In *Dreaming of Hitler: Passions & Provocations.* New York: Crown, 1997, 319-30.

Metzger, Bruce M. *An Introduction to the Apocrypha.* New York: Oxford University Press, 1957.

Miller, Douglas B. "Qohelet's Symbolic Use of הבל." *JBL* 117 (1998): 437-54.

Morgan, Donn F. *Wisdom in the Old Testament Traditions.* Atlanta: John Knox, 1981.

Murphy, Roland E. "Wisdom and Yahwism." In *No Famine in the Land: Studies in Honor of John L. McKenzie,* ed. James W. Flanagan and Anita Weisbrod Robinson. Missoula: Scholars, 1965, 117-26.

―――. "Kerygma of the Book of Proverbs." *Int* 20 (1966): 3-14.

―――. "Assumptions and Problems in Old Testament Wisdom Research." *CBQ* 29 (1967): 101-12.

―――. "The Interpretation of Old Testament Wisdom Literature." *Int* 23 (1969): 289-301.

―――. "What and Where Is Wisdom?" *CurTM* 4 (1977): 283-87.

—————. "Qoheleth's 'Quarrel' with the Fathers." In *From Faith to Faith: Essays in Honor of Donald G. Miller on His Seventieth Birthday,* ed. Dikran Y. Hadidian. PTMS 31. Pittsburgh: Pickwick, 1979, 235-45.

—————. "Hebrew Wisdom." *JAOS* 101 (1981): 21-34.

—————. *Wisdom Literature: Job, Proverbs, Ruth, Canticles, Ecclesiastes, and Esther.* FOTL 13. Grand Rapids: Eerdmans, 1981.

—————. "Wisdom and Creation." *JBL* 104 (1985): 3-11.

—————. "Wisdom and Eros in Proverbs 1–9." *CBQ* 50 (1988): 600-603.

—————. *The Tree of Life: An Exploration of Biblical Wisdom Literature.* ABRL. New York: Doubleday, 1990. 2nd ed. Grand Rapids: Eerdmans, 1996.

—————. "Recent Research on Proverbs and Qoheleth." *CurTM* 1 (1993): 119-40.

Newsom, Carol A. "Job and Ecclesiastes." In *Old Testament Interpretation: Past, Present, and Future: Essays in Honor of Gene M. Tucker,* ed. James Luther Mays, David L. Petersen, and Kent Harold Richards. Nashville: Abingdon, 1995, 177-94.

Nickelsburg, George W. E. *Jewish Literature Between the Bible and the Mishnah: A Historical and Literary Introduction.* Philadelphia: Fortress, 1981.

Ogden, Graham S. *Qoheleth.* 2nd ed. Sheffield: Sheffield Phoenix, 2007.

Patrick, Dale. "Job's Address of God." *ZAW* 91 (1979): 268-82.

Peake, A. S. "Job: The Problem of the Book." In Crenshaw, *Theodicy in the Old Testament,* 100-108.

Peck, Russell A. "Ecclesiastes as a Pivotal Biblical and Literary Text." *ADE Bulletin* 81 (1985): 43-48.

Penchansky, David. *The Betrayal of God: Ideological Conflict in Job.* Louisville: Westminster John Knox, 1990.

—————. *The Politics of Biblical Theology: A Postmodern Reading.* Macon: Mercer University Press, 1995.

—————. "Proverbs." In *Mercer Commentary on the Bible,* ed. Watson E. Mills and Richard F. Wilson. Macon: Mercer University Press, 1995, 193-96.

—————. *What Rough Beast: Images of God in the Hebrew Bible.* Louisville: Westminster John Knox, 1999.

—————. *Twilight of the Gods: Polytheism in the Hebrew Bible.* Louisville: Westminster John Knox, 2005.

—————. "Divine Retribution." In *NIDB,* 2.

Perdue, Leo G. "Wisdom in the Book of Job." In Perdue, Scott, and Wiseman, *In Search of Wisdom,* 73-98.

—————. *The Sword and the Stylus: An Invitation to Wisdom in the Age of Empires.* Grand Rapids: Eerdmans, 2008.

Perdue, Leo G., Bernard Brandon Scott, and William Johnston Wiseman, eds. *In Search of Wisdom: Essays in Memory of John G. Gammie.* Louisville: Westminster John Knox, 1993.

Perry, T. A. *Dialogues with Kohelet: The Book of Ecclesiastes.* University Park: Pennsylvania State University Press, 1993.

Pfeiffer, Robert Henry. "The Peculiar Skepticism of Ecclesiastes." *JBL* 53 (1934): 100-109.

Pixley, Jorge V. "Qoheleth: A Teacher for Our Times." *CurTM* 26 (1999): 123-35.

Polk, Timothy. "The Wisdom of Irony: A Study of *Hebel* and Its Relation to Joy and Fear of God in Ecclesiastes." *SBTh* 6 (1976): 3-17.

Pope, Marvin H. *Job.* AB 15. Garden City: Doubleday, 1973.

Priest, John F. "Humanism, Skepticism, and Pessimism in Israel." *JAAR* 36 (1968): 311-26.

Purvis, James D. "Ben Sira and the Foolish People of Shechem [Sir 50:25-26]." *JNES* 24 (1965): 88-94.

Rad, Gerhard von. *Old Testament Theology.* Trans. D. M. G. Stalker. Edinburgh: Oliver and Boyd and New York: Harper & Row, 1962, 1:152-53.

———. *Wisdom in Israel.* Trans. James D. Marton. London: SCM and Nashville: Abingdon, 1972.

Rankin, O. S. *Israel's Wisdom Literature: Its Bearing on Theology and the History of Religion.* Edinburgh: T. & T. Clark, 1936. Repr. New York: Schocken, 1969.

———. "The Book of Ecclesiastes." In *IB,* 5 (1956): 1-88.

Reese, James Miller. *The Book of Wisdom, Song of Songs.* Old Testament Message 20. Wilmington: Glazier, 1983.

Reymond, Eric. Review of Michael V. Fox, *A Time to Tear Down and a Time to Build Up: A Rereading of Ecclesiastes. JNES* 61 (2002): 319-20.

Ringgren, Helmer. *Word and Wisdom: Studies in the Hypostatization of Divine Qualities and Function in the Ancient Near East.* Lund: Ohlssons, 1947.

Robertson, David A. "The Book of Job: A Literary Study." *Soundings* 56 (1973): 446-69.

———. *The Old Testament and the Literary Critic.* GBS. Minneapolis: Fortress, 1977.

Robinson, H. Wheeler. *Inspiration and Revelation in the Old Testament.* Oxford: Clarendon, 1946.

Rost, Leonhard. *Judaism Outside the Hebrew Canon: An Introduction to the Documents.* Trans. David E. Green. Nashville: Abingdon, 1976.

Roth, Cecil. "Ecclesiasticus in the Synagogue Service." *JBL* 71 (1952): 171-78.

Roth, Wolfgang. "On the Gnomic-Discursive Wisdom of Jesus Ben Sirach." *Semeia* 17 (1980): 59-79.

Rudman, Dominic. "A Contextual Reading of Ecclesiastes 4:13-16." *JBL* 116 (1997): 57-73.

Rylaarsdam, J. Coert. *Revelation in Jewish Wisdom Literature.* Chicago: University of Chicago Press, 1946.

Sanders, Jack T. "Ben Sira's Ethics of Caution." *HUCA* 50 (1979): 73-106.

————. *Ben Sira and Demotic Wisdom.* SBLMS 28. Chico: Scholars, 1983.

Scott, R. B. Y. "Priesthood, Prophecy, Wisdom, and the Knowledge of God." *JBL* 80 (1961): 1-15.

————. *Proverbs. Ecclesiastes.* AB 18. Garden City: Doubleday, 1965.

————. "Wise and Foolish, Righteous and Wicked." In *Studies in the Religion of Israel,* ed. G. W. Anderson. VTSup 23. Leiden: Brill, 1972, 146-65.

————. "Solomon and the Beginnings of Wisdom." In Crenshaw, *Studies in Ancient Israelite Wisdom,* 84-101.

Seow, Choon-Leong. *Ecclesiastes.* AB 18C. New York: Doubleday, 1997.

Seybold, Kiel. הֶבֶל, הָבַל. In *TDOT* 3 (1978): 313-20.

Shapiro, D. "Proverbs." In *Congregation: Contemporary Writers Read the Jewish Bible,* ed. David Rosenberg. New York: Harcourt Brace Jovanovich, 1987, 313-30.

Sharp, Carolyn J. "Ironic Representation, Authorial Voice, and Meaning in Qohelet." *BibInt* 12 (2004): 37-68.

Shead, Andrew G. "Ecclesiastes from the Outside In." *RTR* 55 (1996): 24-37.

————. "Reading Ecclesiastes 'Epilogically.'" *TynBul* 48 (1997): 67-91.

Sheppard, Gerald T. "The Epilogue to Qoheleth as Theological Commentary." *CBQ* 39 (1977): 182-89.

————. "Wisdom and Torah: The Interpretation of Deuteronomy Underlying Sirach 24:23." In *Biblical and Near Eastern Studies: Essays in Honor of William Sanford LaSor,* ed. Gary A. Tuttle. Grand Rapids: Eerdmans, 1978, 166-76.

————. *Wisdom as a Hermeneutical Construct: A Study in the Sapientializing of the Old Testament.* BZAW 151. Berlin: de Gruyter, 1980.

Skehan, Patrick W. *Studies in Israelite Poetry and Wisdom.* CBQMS 1. Washington: Catholic Biblical Association, 1971.

————. "A Single Editor for the Whole Book of Proverbs." In Crenshaw, *Studies in Ancient Israelite Wisdom,* 329-40.

Skehan, Patrick W., and Alexander A. Di Lella. *The Wisdom of Ben Sira.* AB 39. New York: Doubleday, 1987.

Snaith, John G. "Ben Sira's Supposed Love of Liturgy." *VT* 25 (1975): 167-74.

———. "Ecclesiasticus: A Tract for the Times." In *Wisdom in Ancient Israel: Essays in Honour of J. A. Emerton,* ed. John Day, Robert P. Gordon, and H. G. M. Williamson. Cambridge: Cambridge University Press, 1995, 170-81.

Snell, Daniel C., ed. *Twice-Told Proverbs and the Composition of the Book of Proverbs.* Winona Lake: Eisenbrauns, 1993.

Soggin, J. Alberto. *Introduction to the Old Testament: From Its Origins to the Closing of the Alexandrian Canon.* Rev. ed. Trans. John Bowden. OTL. Philadelphia: Westminster, 1980.

Staples, William Ewart. "The 'Vanity' of Ecclesiastes." *JNES* 2 (1943): 95-104.

Terrien, Samuel L. *The Elusive Presence: Toward a New Biblical Theology.* San Francisco: Harper & Row. 1978.

Toy, Crawford H. *A Critical and Exegetical Commentary on the Book of Proverbs.* ICC. Edinburgh: T. & T. Clark, 1959.

Trenchard, Warren C. *Ben Sira's View of Women: A Literary Analysis.* BJS 38. Chico: Scholars, 1982.

Tsevat, Matitiahu. "The Meaning of the Book of Job." *HUCA* 37 (1966): 73-106.

Van Leeuwen, Raymond C.. "The Book of Proverbs." In *The New Interpreter's Bible,* ed. Leander E. Keck. Nashville: Abingdon, 239-48.

Walsh, Jerome T. "Despair as a Theological Virtue in the Spirituality of Ecclesiastes." *BTB* 12 (1982): 46-49.

Washington, Harold C. Review of Martin A. Shields, *The End of Wisdom: A Reappraisal of the Historical and Canonical Function of Ecclesiastes. Review of Biblical Literature* 25.6 (June 2009): 1-4.

Weiss, Meir. *The Story of Job's Beginning: Job 1-2, A Literary Analysis.* Jerusalem: Magnes, 1983.

Whybray, R. N. *The Succession Narrative: A Study of II Samuel 9-20; I Kings 1 and 2.* SBT, 2nd ser. 9. Naperville: Allenson, 1968.

———. *The Intellectual Tradition in Israel.* BZAW 135. Berlin: de Gruyter, 1974.

———. "Qoheleth, Preacher of Joy." *JSOT* 23 (1982): 87-98.

———. *Ecclesiastes.* NCBC. Grand Rapids: Eerdmans and London: Marshall, Morgan & Scott, 1989.

———. *Proverbs.* NCBC. Grand Rapids: Eerdmans, 1994.

Wilckens, Ulrich. σοφία. In *TDNT,* 7 (1971): 465-528.

Williams, James G. "'You Have Not Spoken Truth of Me': Mystery and Irony in Job." *ZAW* 83 (1971): 231-55.

————. "What Does It Profit a Man: The Wisdom of Koheleth." In Crenshaw, *Studies In Ancient Israelite Wisdom*, 375-89.

————. "The Power of Form: A Study of Biblical Proverbs." *Semeia* 17 (1980): 35-58.

Wilson, F. M. "Sacred and Profane? The Yahwistic Redaction of Proverbs Reconsidered." In Hogland et al., *The Listening Heart*, 313-34.

Wilson, Gerald H. "'The Words of the Wise': The Intent and Significance of Qohelet 12:9-14." *JBL* 103 (1984): 175-92.

Winston, David. *The Wisdom of Solomon*. AB 43. Garden City: Doubleday, 1979.

————. "Solomon, Wisdom of." In *ABD*, 6:120-27.

Wolde, Ellen J. Van. "Job 42:1-6: The Reversal of Job." In Beuken, *The Book of Job*, 223-50.

Wright, Addison G. "The Structure of the Book of Wisdom." *Bib* 48 (1967): 165-84.

————. "Riddle of the Sphinx: The Structure of the Book of Qoheleth." *CBQ* 30 (1968): 313-34.

————. "The Riddle of the Sphinx Revisited: Numerical Patterns in the Book of Qoheleth." *CBQ* 42 (1980): 38-51.

Yee, Gale A. "I Have Perfumed My Bed with Myrrh": The Foreign Woman ('iššâ zārâ) in Proverbs 1–9." *JSOT* 43 (1989): 53-68.

Zimmerli, Walther. "The Place and Limit of the Wisdom in the Framework of the Old Testament Theology." *SJT* 17 (1964): 146-58. Repr. in Crenshaw, *Studies in Ancient Israelite Wisdom*, 314-28.

Subject and Author Index

Scripture Index